Country Guitar for Beg

A Complete Method to Learn Traditional and Modern

BY LEVI CLAY

Published by **www.fundamental-changes.com**

ISBN: 978-1-911267-35-5

www.fundamental-changes.com

Twitter: **@guitar_joseph**
Twitter: **@LeviClay88**
Over 7500 fans on Facebook: **FundamentalChangesInGuitar**
Instagram: **FundamentalChanges**

**For over 250 Free Guitar Lessons with Videos Check Out
www.fundamental-changes.com**

Cover Image Copyright: Levi Clay for Fundamental Changes Ltd.

Other Books from Fundamental Changes

The Complete Guide to Playing Blues Guitar Book One: Rhythm Guitar

The Complete Guide to Playing Blues Guitar Book Two: Melodic Phrasing

The Complete Guide to Playing Blues Guitar Book Three: Beyond Pentatonics

The Complete Guide to Playing Blues Guitar Compilation

The CAGED System and 100 Licks for Blues Guitar

Fundamental Changes in Jazz Guitar: The Major ii V I

Minor ii V Mastery for Jazz Guitar

Jazz Blues Soloing for Guitar

Guitar Scales in Context

Guitar Chords in Context

Jazz Guitar Chord Mastery

Complete Technique for Modern Guitar

Funk Guitar Mastery

The Complete Technique, Theory and Scales Compilation for Guitar

Sight Reading Mastery for Guitar

Rock Guitar Un-CAGED: The CAGED System and 100 Licks for Rock Guitar

The Practical Guide to Modern Music Theory for Guitarists

Beginner's Guitar Lessons: The Essential Guide

Chord Tone Soloing for Jazz Guitar

Heavy Metal Rhythm Guitar

Heavy Metal Lead Guitar

Exotic Pentatonic Soloing for Guitar

Heavy Metal Rhythm Guitar

Progressive Metal Guitar

Voice Leading Jazz Guitar

The Complete Jazz Soloing Compilation

The Jazz Guitar Chords Compilation

Fingerstyle Blues Guitar

The Complete DADGAD Guitar Method

Contents

Get the Audio

The audio files for this book are available to download for free from **www.fundamental-changes.com** and the link is in the top right corner. Simply select this book title from the drop-down menu and follow the instructions to get the audio.

We recommend that you download the files directly to your computer, not to your tablet, and extract them there before adding them to your media library. You can then put them on your tablet, iPod or burn them to CD.

On the download page there is a help PDF, and we also provide technical support via the contact form.

Be Social:

For over 250 Free Guitar Lessons with Videos Check out:
www.fundamental-changes.com

Twitter: **@guitar_joseph**
Twitter: **@LeviClay88**
Over 7500 fans on FaceBook: **FundamentalChangesInGuitar**
Instagram: **FundamentalChanges**

Introduction

Considered by many to be the sound of America, surveys will tell you that there's no more popular genre of music than country music. Country and Western has a rich history, but to many only conjures up images of cowboys. However, the reality is that there's so much more to the story than this.

Born in the 1920s, country music shares many similarities with the blues, in that country is a fusion of music from other continents that found a footing in a new location. While we might think of the birthplace of the genre as the Appalachian Mountains, many would argue that the music was actually conceived in in the traditional folk sound and instrumentation of countries like Ireland and Scotland.

After many generations in the Appalachian melting pot (where music was played socially for entertainment), residents began to move south to work in cities like Atlanta, Georgia. This brought country music to ears of a different type of person; the business man. It was here that the recording industry would start to experiment with the commercial potential of country music. By the end of the '20s, the American people would come to know these early country sounds through success stories such as Jimmie Rodgers and The Carter Family.

During the '30s, the Great Depression saw a dramatic drop in record sales. The solution for music lovers was the radio renaissance, with the Grand Ole Opry filling the ears of anyone willing to listen. Thanks to Hollywood, the idea of the cowboy ballad caught on, with artists like Roy Acuff having hits with classics such as Wabash Cannonball.

Things really changed in the 1940s as western swing took off, with Bob Wills and his Texas Playboys bringing amplified electric guitar and even drums into his band. This may sound trivial now, but at the time these changes were revolutionary and despised by purists. Simultaneously there was an explosion in the bluegrass scene, as Bill Monroe and the Blue Grass Boys took the traditional unamplified folk and gospel music to new commercial heights.

Country music would continue to grow and branch into numerous sub-genres over the next sixty years, not to mention become one of the driving sounds behind rockabilly, and eventually, rock and roll. From the ballads of Hank Williams to the stardom of Johnny Cash... the simple sounds of Merle Travis to the sophistications of Chet Atkins... the class of Merle Haggard to the rebellion of Willie Nelson... the pop of Dolly Parton to the rock of the Allman Brothers... or the traditions of Alan Jackson verses the progression of Carrie Underwood: Country music is a genre you could spend a long time getting to know, as it runs deep in the DNA of the music of the 20th century.

Country guitar is a fascinating genre and will require serious dedication and passion to achieve the mastery of Albert Lee or Brent Mason's hot licks. On the other hand, it's very easy to achieve a good command of the genre by playing songs and solos typical of the style.

I really do believe that Scotty Anderson may be one of the most terrifyingly technical players to ever pick up the guitar, and this should come as no surprise when you hear the playing of Jimmy Bryant, way back in the '50s; long before 'shred' guitar appeared!

If you want to get technical, then stick at it, but remember that the foundations of timing, tone and stylistic awareness are the bedrock on which these skills should be built.

Country Guitar for Beginners is split into two sections that are designed to develop the specific skills needed to become proficient in the many elements of the genre.

Part One focuses on chord playing and rhythm guitar skills. By developing a good feel now, you will sit tightly on the groove later when you're running up and down the neck with open string cascades and punchy double stops. Remember, the guitar didn't really function as a lead instrument until much later in the genre's development. It's all well and good being able to play Hot Wired (in fact it's pretty impressive!), but you also need to be able to know how to play something like Hey Good Lookin' or San Antonio Rose when required.

Once you've completed Part One, you will be ready to play anything you'd hear from Jimmie Rodgers, Hank Williams, Johnny Cash or similar icons of the genre. Building a sense of this style is imperative if you want to study players like Chet Atkins or the great Jerry Reed.

Part Two takes you through everything you need to play lead guitar solos typical of the earlier styles of country music. You'll look at basic picking concepts and how to *flat pick* and *thumb pick*… how to embellish rhythm parts with typical double stop riffs… scales in multiple keys… the use of triads as soloing guides… bending ideas, diatonic intervals and arpeggios. The goal is to teach you to fill the shoes of legendary guitarists like Roy Nichols, James Burton, Luther Perkins, and Eldon Shamblin.

While your ultimate goal may be to become the next Danny Gatton or Johnny Hiland, never lose sight of the roots. There's a reason these guys sound wonderful, and it's their understanding of everything that country music is. They don't sound like rock players who learned a few old country clichés.

At times, this journey may seem tough, but speaking as someone who got into country music relatively late in my life, I can say with absolute confidence that your skills will develop in time. Take it slow and make sure every movement is calm and calculated.

Remember the old adage: don't practice until you get it right, practice until you can't get it wrong. Stick at it, and with slow repetition, you're sure to get where you want to be.

Music isn't just about where you're going; it's about enjoying the journey.

Have fun,

Levi

Part One: Chords and Rhythm Guitar

In this section, you'll revisit the essential chord voicings found in everything from cowboy ballads to western swing. You may know some of these chords already but don't skip them as everything will matter by the time you reach the end of the chapter. There are plenty of country guitar secrets thrown in too... so pay attention! Once you've refreshed these voicings, you will look at the many ways they're used in real country rhythm guitar.

This section covers:

- Many usable chord diagrams
- Tips for changing chords
- Rhythm counting exercises
- Common chord progressions
- 'Alternating Bass' strumming
- Theory of chord construction
- Western Swing-style chord voicings
- Adding jazz influences
- Inversions and applications
- Western Swing chord progressions
- Modern strumming patterns

By mastering the skills in this section, you'll prepare yourself to dig deeper into other areas. Along with building dexterity in the fretting hand, you'll build the skills needed to tackle lead guitar too.

While it may be tempting to skip over some of these sections if you are a more advanced player remember that your sense of groove and timekeeping can *always* be improved, and the most efficient way to develop your abilities is by locking in with a good rhythm part and stay in the zone for hours.

The rhythm guitar skills we're looking at in part one are the ones most often required for singers and band work. So once you've got these rhythms and chords solid, try playing with a singer, or sing a melody yourself. Your focus should always be the music, and as you become more comfortable with these rhythms, you'll find yourself free to listen when playing.

I promise you'll thank me later!

Chapter One: Country Chord Refresher

At this stage, I assume that you're already familiar with basic open chords and some simple chord progressions, but really *understanding* these chords is the key to success in country guitar. Ignoring this aspect of music would be akin to building a house without foundations; everything may appear fine, but it could collapse at any time.

It would not be an understatement to say that chord knowledge is the most important aspect of playing country guitar - not just as a rhythm player, but as a lead guitarist too.

Before we begin, I want you to play a note on the guitar, absolutely any note, and ask yourself, "is this a good note?".

The answer is always "eh?!".

It's a question that doesn't make any sense because a single note is nothing without context. If I play the note A against an A chord, it sounds fine. If I play that same A against an F chord it sounds great too. If I play that same A against a G# chord, it normally sounds pretty awful! The distances between these notes are called intervals.

The lesson is that in music, everything is intervals. Even in the key of E, the E won't sound great over every chord. Some intervals are pleasing to the ear, and others are less effective.

It's important to learn about chords because this knowledge will give you great insight into which notes will sound good, and which notes won't.

First, let's look at five of the most common Major chords found in country music. These crop up often in songs in the keys of C, G, D and even F.

In these early diagrams, I've included finger numbers to show you how these are often played. 1 represents the index finger, 2 is the middle finger and so on.

I've included these fingerings as most guitarists *don't* finger the G Major chord this way. It may feel a little uncomfortable at first, but it works great when combined with the C Major chord.

The fingering for F Major is also an eye-opener to many students who are used to a six-string barre. However, this 'mini-barre' is how Jimmie Rodgers would have played the chord. Understanding that this is a completely acceptable way to play the chord will come in handy later on when you're playing chord voicings common in Merle Travis or Chet Atkins style.

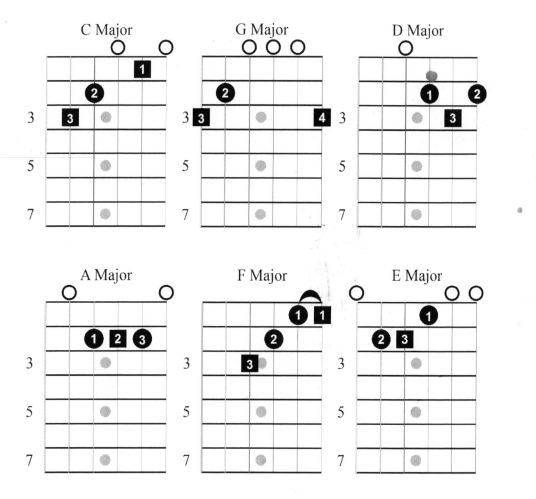

If you combine some of these chords into a simple progression, you're able to practice both timing and fretting-hand dexterity.

Your first goal is to move each of your fingers from one chord to the next simultaneously, rather than one at a time, as this can result in a perceptible delay in the chord changes.

The only way to master any chord is by building *muscle memory*, so take time to look at the previous diagrams and see each chord as a whole unit in your mind before placing your fingers on the guitar. Slowly practice forming each chord from nothing. Take your hand off the fingerboard, move to the chord, take your hand off the neck and repeat.

Time in music is divided into bars. Each bar of music contains four beats, and in the following examples, each chord lasts for two of those beats. As we count 1, 2, 3, 4, we're going to play a chord on both beat 1 and beat 3. The most important tip I can give here is that your strumming arm should be used as a time keeping device, so your arm moves up and down on every beat. This process begins as I count in with the metronome, so my first strum will be placed accurately on beat 1.

Always strum the beats (1, 2, 3 and 4) with a down strum. Notes that fall between the beats will be played with an up-strum.

Example 1a:

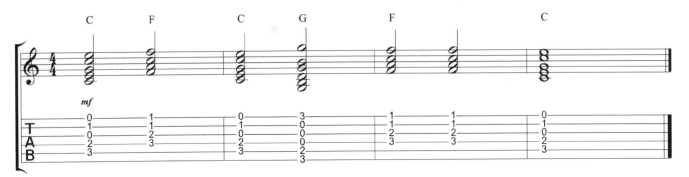

Let's look at simple variations to these chords that will turn them from *Major* chords into *Dominant* chords.

We learn the theory of this when we discuss Western swing later, but at this stage, it's important to train the fingers and the ears without complicating the music with theory. It's more important to be able to *hear* the difference between Major and Dominant chords, so when you play the Dominant chords try to describe in words how it *sounds* to you.

There are no wrong answers! It's all about associating an idea or feeling with the sound of a Dominant chord so that it jumps out at you when you hear it.

Play through the following Dominant chords. In most cases, there is only one note different between the Major and Dominant versions of each chord.

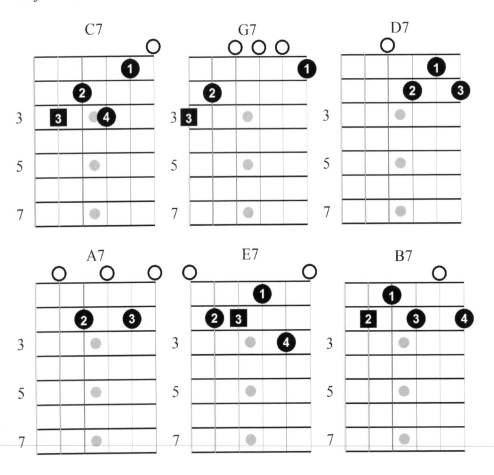

As with the Major chords, we can use these new chords in a progression to learn how they function, and to give our fingers a chance to start moving between them.

Example 1b:

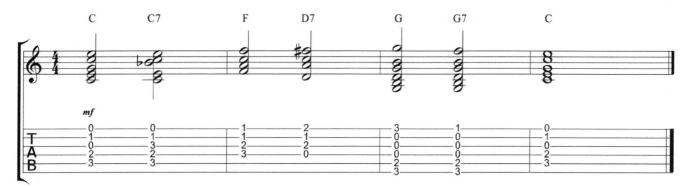

Next, we will learn some Minor chords.

To me, these chords sound "sad" or perhaps "longing"… but that's just me! The ultimate goal is to be able to *hear* these chords and say, "oh, that's a Minor chord!".

Practice changing between the following chords.

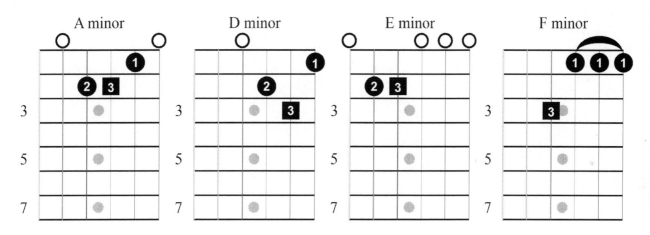

Now we can start to combine all the different chord types to create a chord *progression*.

This example contains some strumming. In this example, there are four chord strums per bar, and each is played with a down-stroke. Many more strumming ideas will be covered in the next chapter.

The following country ballad can be played very slowly and the key is to lock into the metronome by strumming a chord each time the metronome clicks. Count this out loud as, "1, 2, 3, 4, 1, 2, 3, 4". This is referred to as 4/4, or *common* time, with each beat being a 1/4 note (as it takes up 1/4 of a 4/4 bar).

Example 1c:

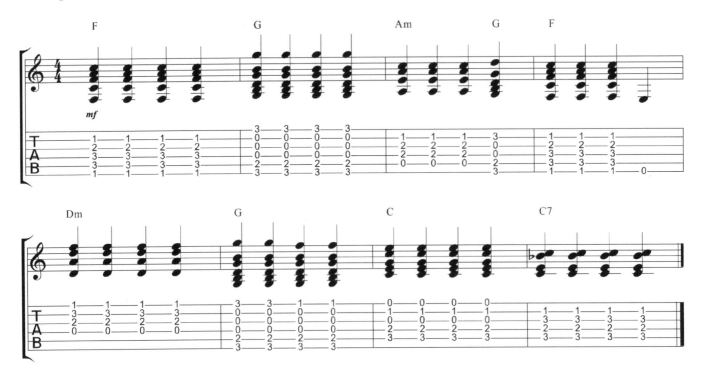

Early country music was closely related to gospel music. Amazing Grace is a wonderful hymn dating back as far as 1779. We play it here in the key of G and use a mixture of Major, Minor and Dominant chords.

Unlike the previous example, this piece has a 'three' feel, meaning there are three beats in each bar. Count "1, 2, 3, 1, 2, 3", and accent the first beat a little louder to help keep the feel.

I encourage you to sing the melody if you're familiar with it. It's surprising how complete a chord progression like this can feel just by adding the melody.

Example 1d:

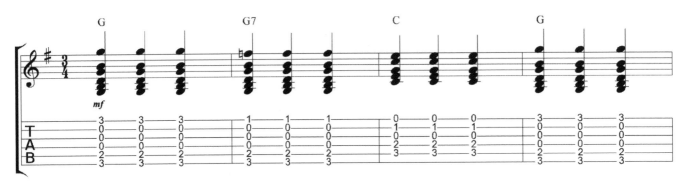

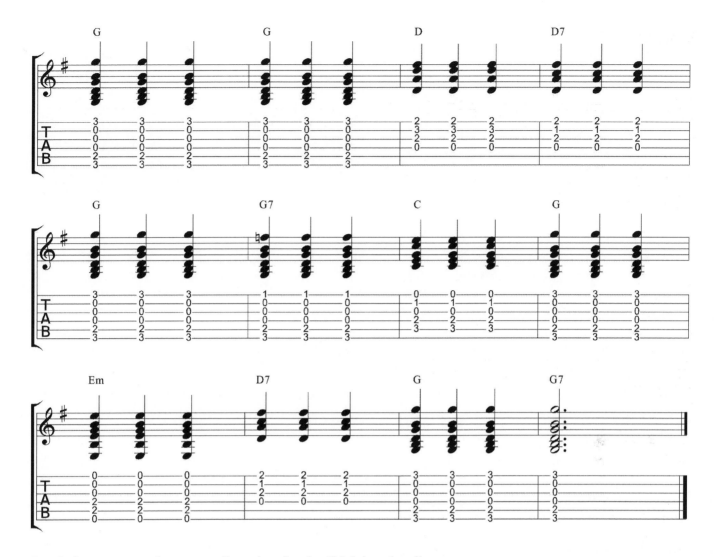

Don't forget to use the proper fingering for the G Major chord!

The intention here is to demonstrate how these simple chords can form the basis of many songs. Using them shouldn't be looked down on in any way.

Take the time to practice these simple chord progressions and attempt to distinguish the difference in sound between each chord family (Major, Minor, Dominant). I find the best way to do this is to play the chord progressions so slowly that I am able to think ahead. When playing the G Major chord from the previous example, I attempt to 'hear' what the G7 chord is going to sound like in my mind before I play it. Focusing on these harmonic shifts is one of the best ways to train your ears.

Chapter Two: Basic Strumming and Playing Songs

Now you know some chords, let's use them to make music in the style of the early country players.

The first thing to consider is the *function* of the guitar in country music; how it developed, and what is required to create an authentic sound when backing a singer or creating a rhythm track.

As mentioned in the introduction, drums in country music didn't occur until many years after the genre had taken off, and even then it was something the purists were adamantly against. There are stories of the Grand Ole Opry refusing to let artists use drums, despite there being a drummer in their band. This essentially cut out a huge avenue of exposure for any artist trying to move with the times by bringing in pop or rock influences, rather than sticking true to a 'pure' genre that was dwindling in popularity.

The period without drums resulted in the other instruments having to create a driving, percussive sound in other ways. As such, the guitar acted as both an instrument that provided harmony, and a percussive instrument to keep time so that people could dance. One might argue that the guitar is best used as a source of percussion because many country bands (especially in Honky-Tonk bars) had pianos which always outclassed guitars as harmony providers.

The 'classic' country feel that developed was a combination of the bass playing on beats 1 and 3 of the bar with a heavy accent on the guitar on beats 2 and 4. This 2 and 4 accent is commonly known as a *backbeat*, and is the defining sound in contemporary 4/4 music, from early jazz, right up to the pop music of today.

Let's recreate this feel on a C Major chord to really get the effect locked in our ears and muscles. To keep the playing interesting, we'll imitate what a bass player would play on our lowest strings.

Listen closely to the recording of the following example because the *dynamics* are important. We'll begin by playing the root note on beat 1, then a chord on beat 2. Next, we play the 5th degree of C Major (G)[1] and then accent the chord again on beat 4.

Repeat this sequence repeats as long as is required to commit it to muscle memory. Take your time with this example and get comfortable with the alternating bass note.

Example 2a:

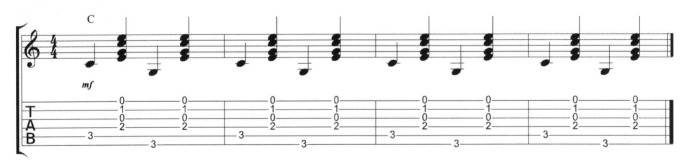

---

[1] The note G is the fifth note in the scale of C Major: C, D, E, F, G.

This movement of the root, followed by the 5th is extremely important in country music. To find the 5th of a chord simply count up five notes from the root. The 5th of A is E (A, B, C, D, E), the 5th of G is D (G, A, B, C, D) etc.

When we change from the C Major chord to the A Major chord, everything in the strumming pattern remains the same, with the root on the fifth string and the 5th on the sixth string. This needs a little more care though, as you don't want the bass notes to ring out into each other. Try to cut off the bass notes with the palm of the strumming hand before hitting the chord stabs.

In bar three and four, the A chord changes to an A7. As this is still an "A-type" chord, the alternating bass pattern doesn't need to change.

Example 2b:

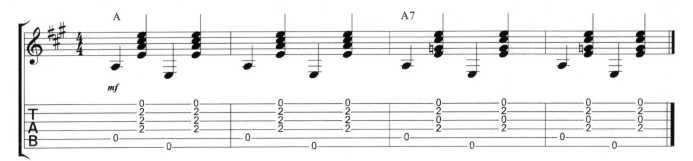

One last example of the root and 5th movement is the following B7 chord. Assuming you've got to grips with the fingering of this chord from the previous chapter, all you need to do is alternate the 2nd finger between the fifth and sixth string. As with the previous chords, move between the root (B) and the 5th (F#). You may notice that if the root of the chord is on the A string, then the 5th will always be on the same fret of the E string.

Example 2c:

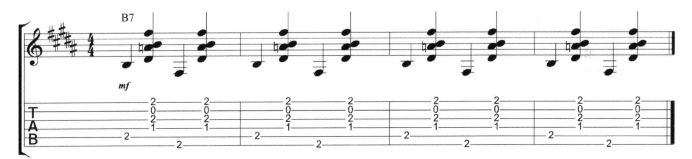

One challenging part of this style is that not all chords have the root on the A string!

This is demonstrated with a G Major chord. With this chord, the root note is on the low E string, and the 5th (D) is on the open D string. This means jumping over the A string to the D string to play the alternating bass. Skipping over the A string can feel awkward at first, but this is an important movement to master.

As with the A Major chord, switch to the Dominant chord in bars three and four.

Example 2d:

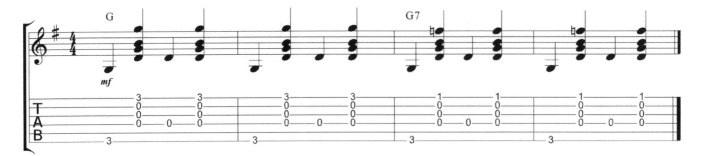

On an E Major chord, the root is on the low E string, and the 5th is on the A string. Moving between these notes will probably feel easy after working on the G chord. As with the previous examples, changing to the Dominant chord in bar three shows you the alternating bass pattern remains consistent here.

Example 2e:

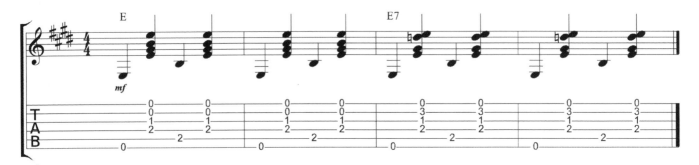

D Major chords have root notes on the open D (fourth) string, and the 5th is played on the open A (fifth) string.

Example 2f:

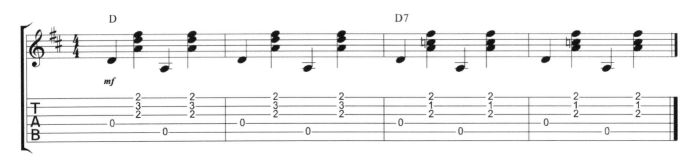

When I really got into playing country rhythm seriously, I noticed that many of the greats would play a 'mini barre' version of the F Major chord, with a root on the D string instead of the low E string. Aside from being easier on the hand than the full barre chord, this voicing also has the benefit of allowing an easy movement to play the 5th on the A string.

Example 2h:

To add more life to these parts, let's develop the backbeat by adding by adding another strum on the upstroke of beats 2 and 4. This creates a count of "1, 2&, 3, 4&, 1, 2&, 3, 4&". The important thing to understand is that the movement in the strumming hand shouldn't change. Continue to strum down on each beat but now simply catch the strings with the pick on the way up too.

Play the previous strumming pattern applied to a C Major and C7 chord.

Example 2i:

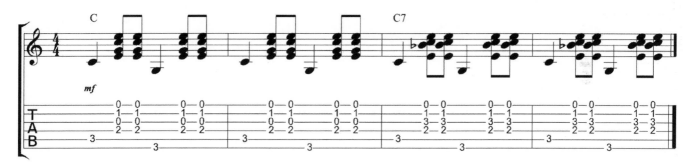

Let's use the previous exercises to make some music! This example is typical of Johnny Cash's approach to rhythm guitar on songs like Walk the Line or Folsom Prison Blues. Johnny was one of the most iconic, best-selling country artists of all time, and his music still touches millions of people the world over, even after his death in 2003.

The chord progression is very close to a standard twelve-bar blues but with a pause on the V chord (B7) for two bars. The bass movement sticks to the root and 5th movement you've just spent time mastering.

Example 2j:

Next, let's add the 'down up' stroke on beat 2 to make a rhythm that is typical of Hank Williams.

As with the previous examples, continue to alternate between the root and the 5th in the bass part to create a solid, driving sound. This is an essential part of the genre, and an important feel to master before moving on to look at the style of legends such as Merle Travis or Chet Atkins.

Example 2k:

The next example is in the style of Jimmie Rodgers, and similar to his playing on classics such as Blue Yodel No.1, or Waiting on a Train.

This example has the same feel as before, but now with added bass notes other than the root and 5th.

Beat 3 of bar two sees you playing the 3rd (E) of the C7 chord. There are no hard and fast rules for choosing these bass notes; it's all about creating an interesting melodic movement to keep the song moving forward. All these extra bass notes simply happen to be within easy reach of the chord fingering.

Example 21:

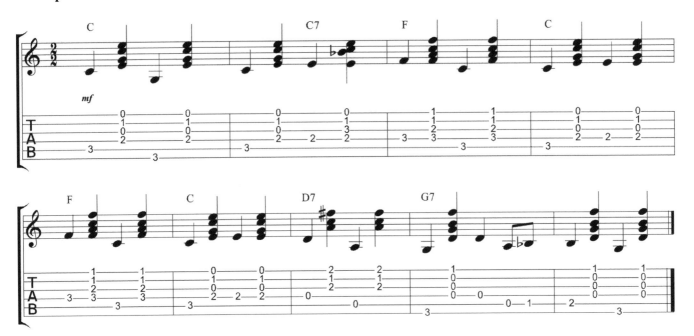

Let's stick with Jimmie's approach to rhythm, but this time play in 3/4. This feel is similar to Amazing Grace from Chapter One, but now you will play a bass note on beat 1 and chord strums on beats 2 and 3.

In this example you'll notice some interesting notes added in the bass, in particular the B played against the C Major chord (bar seven) and the F# played against the G Major chord (bar fifteen). As a rule, you can always approach any chord from a fret below and it's going to sound great.

Example 2m:

You should now be getting a sense of how to create a country backbeat by accenting beat 2 of the bar with a slightly harder strum. If not, listen carefully to the audio examples and try to mimic my playing. This feel is the life-blood of country rhythm guitar, so listen to as much music as you can and try to emulate this feel in your playing.

Syncopation is the act of offsetting a beat so an accent falls somewhere it would not normally be expected.

In reality, this is simply displacing a chord or note that you would expect to fall on a strong beat. On paper, this idea may sound complicated, but it's actually something you'll have heard hundreds of times.

The first syncopated example accents a chord played on the "and" of beat 4. This is held though beat 1 of the following bar.

Remember, the strumming technique here is identical to before. Your hand moves down on the beats and up between the beats. The trick is to keep your hand moving all the time, even though you're not actually striking the strings on beat 1 of bar two.

Keep a strong backbeat by accenting the 2 and 4 where possible. The exception is when you're syncopating, as it sounds best to accent the notes that are off the beat as it helps to make the music sound more human, and less mechanical. My best advice here is to listen to the audio examples: These ideas look complicated on paper but make much more sense once you hear them. Learning music is all about listening and copying what you hear.

Example 2n:

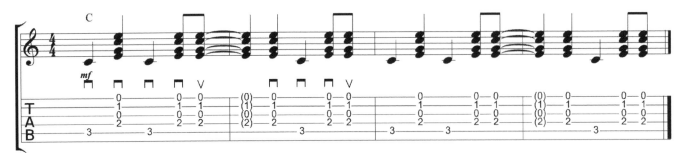

The next example takes the previous idea but moves the syncopated chord to the "and" of beat 2.

You can vocalise bar one by saying; "1, 2 & ... & 4". This counting looks quite complex when written down, so listen closely to the audio example and you'll soon realize this is a rhythm you hear all the time,

Practice this rhythm on the first two bars of the following example. When you start to get the idea, add the second two bars which contain an F Major chord to keep you on your toes.

Example 2o:

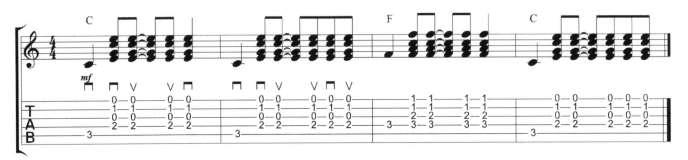

The 3rd example places the syncopated strum on the "and" of beat 2 moving into beat 3.

This rhythm could just as easily be played in the second half of the bar to fall on the "and" of beat 3 moving into beat 4.

It is important to notice that this example affects the backbeat because the syncopated note effectively moves the beat 2 accent earlier than expected.

As always, listen carefully to the audio recording to get a feel for this example. It's always easier to hear these ideas than to learn them by reading.

Example 2p:

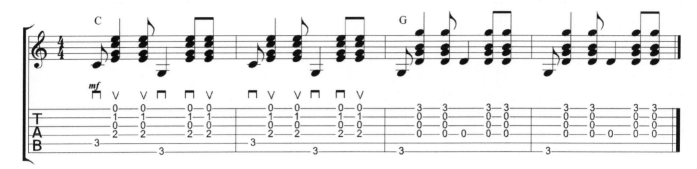

The final example in this chapter applies syncopated ideas to a common country chord progression.

Played in G, the example begins on the I chord (G Major) before moving to the IV (C Major) then V (D Major), this idea then repeats but moves from the V (D Major) to the IV (C Major).

The second section moves to the vi (Em) followed by the V (D Major), this repeats but is varied by a syncopated V7 chord (D7) that pulls you back home to G Major.

Example 2q:

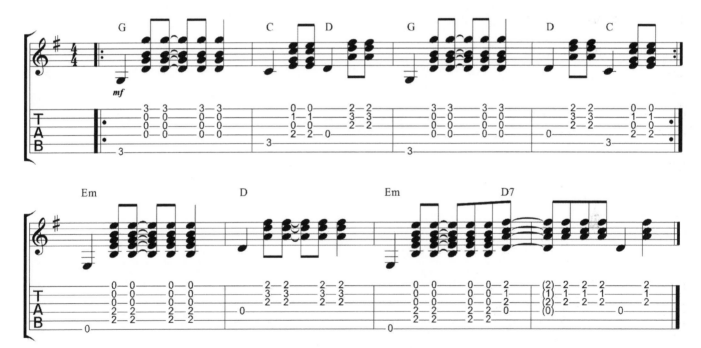

After working through this chapter, you will be armed with the tools to play most common country acoustic strumming parts. You should now be able to explore more rhythm playing and develop your inner pulse while working on simple tunes.

Listen to the country greats and imitate their strumming patterns. The more you listen to legends like Merle Haggard, Waylon Jennings, David Allan Coe, Ernest Tubb and Glen Campbell, the more you'll develop a feel for how these guys played.

What you'll quickly learn is that once you've really mastered strumming, you don't improve by *thinking* more. The best way to improve is by *listening* and *replicating* what you hear. Remember, the strumming hand moves down and up to the music, simply hit the strings as and when you want to hear them.

Chapter Three: Western Swing Rhythm

During the late '20s and early '30s, a new sub-genre of country music began to evolve when the jazz music of the era met the instrumentation of country music found in the South.

Suddenly, bands popped up all over the country playing this new *Western Swing* music for people to dance to. Notable pioneers like Bob Wills, Milton Brown, and Spade Cooley began using drums to add excitement to their driving jazz-based rhythm sections. They were still playing songs, but the more involved chord changes gave guitarists like Eldon Shamblin, Jimmy Wyble, and Junior Barnard something new to experiment with in both their rhythm style and their solos (which were plentiful!).

Unfortunately, the genre saw a sharp decline in the '40s when the US introduced a nightclub tax for "dancing nightclubs" to help raise funds for the war effort. This steep 30% tax saw countless clubs ban dancing, which was enough to all but kill the movement. While the genre never saw a true renaissance, it lived on in the works of bands like The Hot Club of Cowtown, The Lucky Stars, and The Swing Commanders.

One of the defining aspects of Western swing rhythm playing is the driving 'four on the floor' rhythm (four 1/4 notes per measure) and almost dizzying use of chord *inversions*; think Freddie Green in Count Basie Orchestra's Orchestra or Django Reinhardt's rhythm work, but with a redneck twist.

A chord inversion is a voicing where a note *other than the root* note appears in the bass. So while a G Major triad contains the notes G, B, and D, this could be played with any of the three different notes (G, B or D) in the bass; each being a different inversion.

A G Major chord with the root in the bass (G, B, D) is called a *root position chord*.

Playing the 3rd in the bass (B, G, D, or B, D, G) is a *1st inversion* triad and is written as G/B (pronounced 'G over B' and meaning a G chord over a B bass note).

Playing the 5th in the bass gives you a *2nd inversion* triad of G/D.

Example 3a demonstrates three inversions of a G chord beginning with an E-shape barre form.

Each voicing contains just three notes, the root, 5th, and 3rd. This is an open-voiced triad, sometimes called a 'shell voicing'. Stripped down voicings like this have two advantages: not only do they sit well in this musical setting, but using fewer notes makes changing between voicings at faster tempos much easier.

In the following diagrams, the notes that are played are shown as black dots, while the bigger barre chord 'CAGED' shape is shown with hollow notes to give you some context. Don't play the hollow notes.

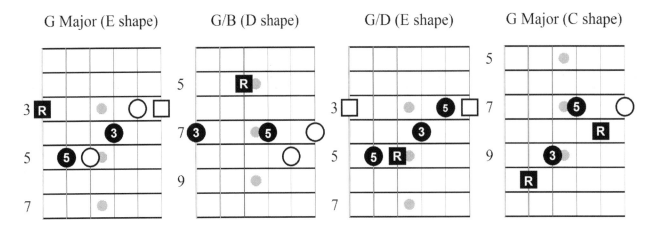

Example 3a:

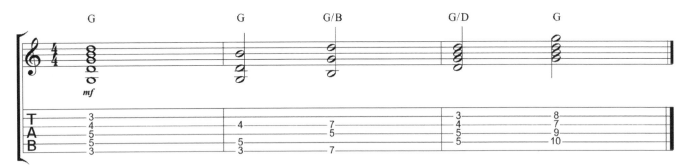

In swing, inversions are used in two ways. While they are used to create smooth changes from chord to chord, they're also used to create interest for the listener when one chord is held for a prolonged period of time. The Bob Wills classic 'Stay a Little Longer' is a good example, as it begins with four bars of a G Major chord. The following example demonstrates how four bars of G Major might be played in *early* country music

Example 3b:

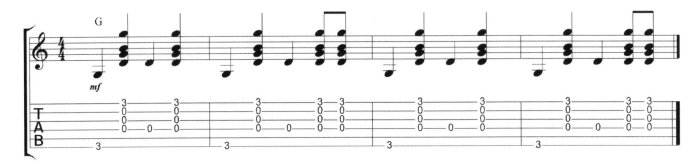

The next example takes that G Major chord but this time moves between some of the inversions above to create interest. Not only are parts like these both fun and challenging to play, they also sound great too.

Example 3c:

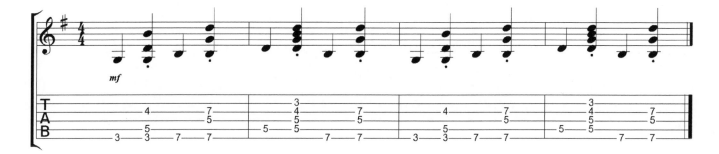

Example 3d demonstrates how a swing player might approach a long stint on one chord. When you look closely, you'll notice this riff contains a melody in the bass. This helps tie the part together and make it feel more like a riff than a stream of chord changes.

Also, the rhythm has been notated a bit literally here, so it's important to get a feel for the dynamics of this style by listening to the audio. There's also definitely a lot of cross-pollination with the famous Gypsy jazz 'la pompe' rhythm. Use a heavy accent on beats 2 and 4, so much so that beats 1 and 3 often only include a single note.

Don't take this too literally! The idea is to have a small, soft strum followed by a bigger, more aggressive strum to push the beat along. Listen to the audio carefully to hear for this yourself.

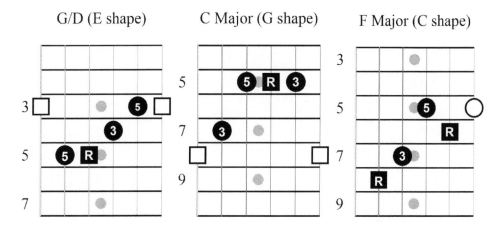

Note the melody in the lowest part of the chords above. While the C/E and F aren't inversions of G, the movement in the bass ties them together nicely.

Example 3d:

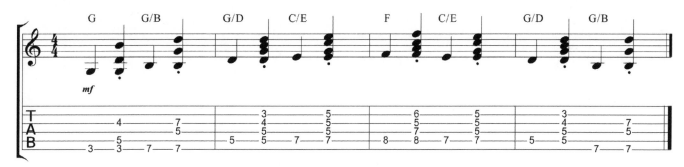

Aside from these fast-paced inversions, Western swing chord vocabulary also contains more extensions, such as 7th- and 6th-chords. As time goes by you'll learn more chord extensions, but the following basic sounds will always serve you well.

Example 3e:

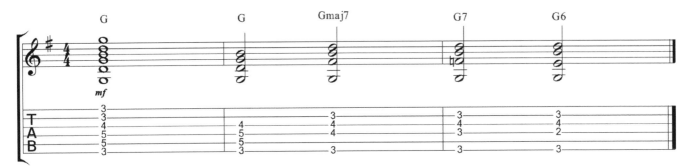

The next example showcases how a swing player might use these sounds when comping on a blues. The first four measures sit on a G Major, but the inner voice of the chords changes the chord from a G Major to a Gmaj7 to a G6 to a G7 which finally resolves to a C7 in bar five. On the return to G Major, there's a repeat of the three inversions studied earlier.

Example 3f:

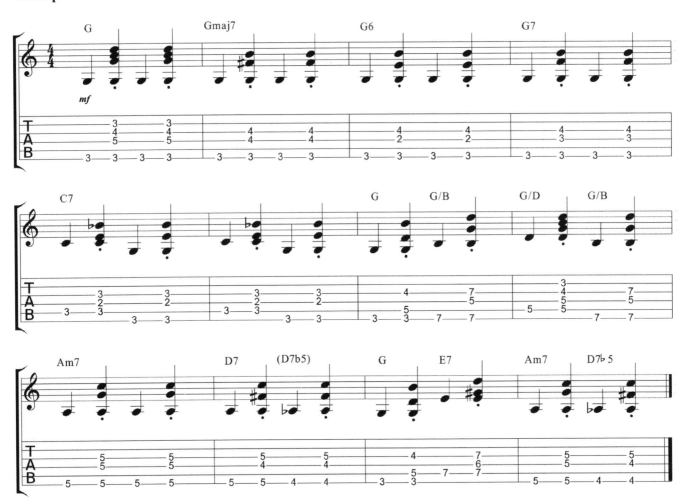

There are also useful inversions and extensions that fit under the hands with an 'A shape' chord While this collection of chords isn't comprehensive, it's certainly enough to draw a decent amount of ideas for a C Major barre chord.

Example 3g:

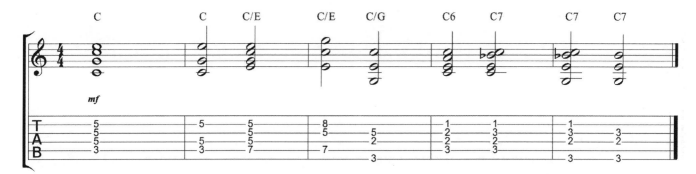

One of the most intriguing parts of swing players is how they're able to create both motion on a static chord, but also connect chord changes fluently. In the following example, begin on a G Major chord and move up the neck using inversions. The transition to the C Major happens via a G7 chord, before moving down the neck in inversions and resolving to the original G Major chord.

Example 3h:

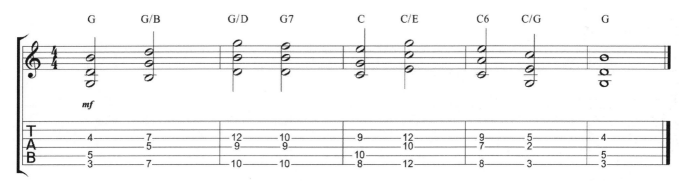

Another common approach that creates harmonic interest is playing chord-scales. The next example features voicings for chords in the key of G Major. Note the use of the C6 in measure two as a sweeter sound than the expected Cmaj7.

Example 3i:

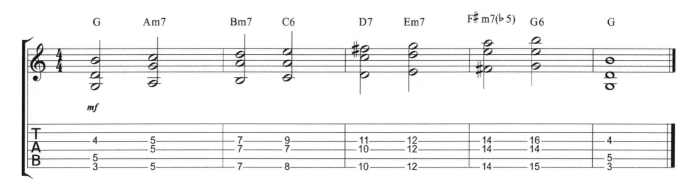

The next example shares many chords with the previous *chord-scale* idea, but instead of playing chords like Bm7 and D7, these have been replaced inversions of the G Major triad and results in the same bass movement, but stays strongly related to the original G Major chord.

Example 3j:

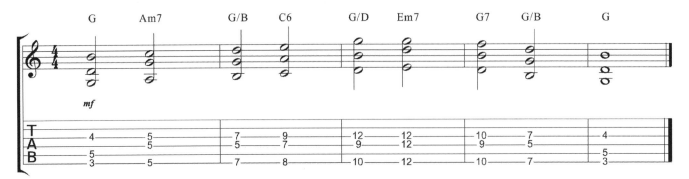

Another common trick is to play *diminished chords a semitone below the chord* they're moving to. For example, playing a G#dim7 between the chords of G Major and Am7. This creates a very smooth transition between the voicings.

As a general rule, you can always play a diminished 7 chord a semitone below the root of the chord you are moving to.

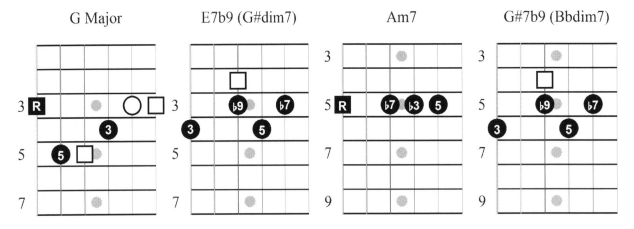

Example 3k:

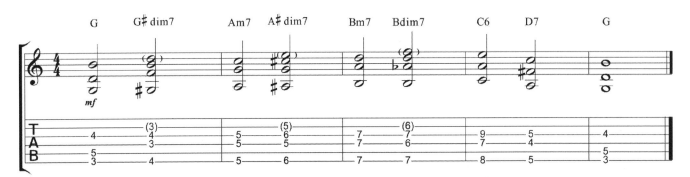

Here's an example of that idea used to create a chord riff on a C Major vamp. First, the C Major moves up the chord-scale to Dm7 (via a diminished chord), then up to a C/E via another diminished chord. This then moves down via a ii-V (Dm7 - G7) back to C Major to turn the riff around. You'll find ideas like this all over Light Crust Doughboys recordings.

This all sounds very complicated, but the important part is to listen to the bass movement and treat it as a melody rather than a complex collection of substitutions and theory.

Example 3l:

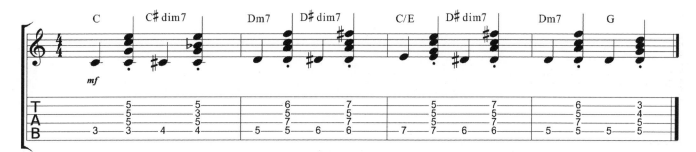

Next is a similar idea, but this time on the lowest strings and in the key of G Major.

Example 3m:

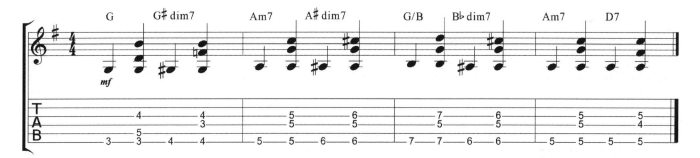

Here's an example similar to something the great Eldon Shamblin might have played. Eldon's work with Bob Wills and His Texas Playboys is a shining example of the style. This idea contains some new chords, including a tricky voicing for G7, and an Eb6. Both of these voicings are based on a C Major barre.

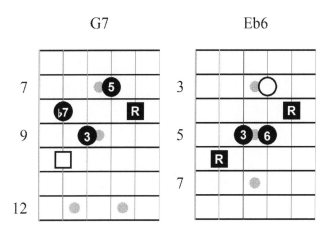

Beginning with a G Major triad, G7 is formed by moving the root note down two frets to the b7, and creating a G7/F. By itself, this voicing it pretty hard on the ears, but sandwiched between the G Major and C/E, the F in the bass works well as it walks down the scale.

Example 3n:

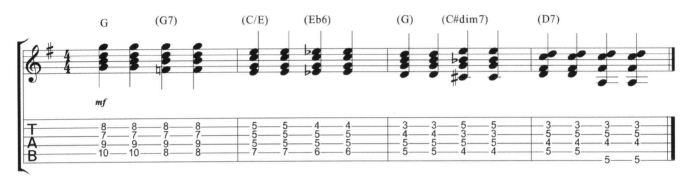

The final example is a little more in-depth, and outlines a sixteen-bar Western swing-type progression. The chord progression in the first four measures could be thought of as G - A7 - D7 - G7 - E7 - A7 D7, but with the guitar playing two chords per bar, and running up and down the neck, things get interesting quite quickly.

Over the G Major chord, a chord-scale approach has been used which contrasts with the inversions played over the A7 chord.

Over the D Major chord we play a walk-down in the bass, starting with the root (D), and moving through the b7, 6th, and 5th.

For the turnaround, we begin with G Major, then move up to a 2nd inversion E7 voicing. This voicing moves down chromatically to return to G Major.

The second eight bars starts with the same movement of G Major to A7. A new trick is shown on the A7 chord, simply move the chord down one fret and back up again! This doesn't need a theoretical explanation; it just sounds great!

The final four bars feature another walk down in the bass, this time beginning on an Em7 chord. To end there is a 'ii-V-I' in G, ending on a clichéd 6/9 voicing that is common in country and early rockabilly music.

Example 3o:

These examples should open your ears up to the sound of this exciting and unique genre of music.

Spend some time listening to the music of Bob Wills and His Texas Playboys, and Milton Brown and His Musical Brownies to become familiar with the standards of the genre. You'll also hear a lot of cross-pollination with the Gypsy Jazz music of Django Reinhardt and the Quintette du Hot Club de France as songs like "After You've Gone" were played by both.

This genre of music influences music that came years later, such as the much beloved Bakersfield sound, that used swing as a main component. Buck Owens would become well known for this music, and players like Vince Gill keep it alive today with his band, The Time Jumpers.

Chapter Four: Hybrid Picking Riffs

After Rock and Roll took over the world and Rockabilly (itself coming from a portamento of rock and hillbilly) gained a cult following, Nashville began producing music with commercial success at the top its the list of priorities. The pop element of country music certainly wasn't a bad thing as it introduced acts like Glen Campbell and Dolly Parton to wider audiences of young people who didn't want to listen to the same music as their parents.

As time went by, more and more flavours were brought to country music and were adapted to country's traditional tastes. No influence was stronger than the mildly overdriven guitar sounds of rock music. This influence went both ways, as rock acts like the Rolling Stones, The Allman Brothers, Lynyrd Skynyrd and The Eagles started using more country-influence ideas. This sound is still strong today, even in the more pop-focused songs of Brad Paisley, Miranda Lambert, and Carrie Underwood

Eventually incorporation of rock into country led to *Truck-Driving* country music, that combined elements of Outlaw, Rock, Honky-Tonk and Bakersfield to create a sound that formed an exciting direction for established artists like Merle Haggard and Jerry Reed, while also creating a vehicle for artists like Alan Jackson and Junior Brown to reach a new audience of their own.

A big part of playing this style authentically is the use of the pick and fingers together, commonly known as *hybrid* picking. Not only does hybrid picking make some things technically easier to play, it also sounds quite different. With hybrid picking, you can play more than one note simultaneously, rather than slightly apart (which is impossible to avoid when strumming with a pick). Hybrid picking also adds a little more 'spank' to the notes as you pull the strings away from the fretboard… After they're plucked, they slap back aggressively against the fretboard.

First up, let's get used to how hybrid picking sounds and feels. Play this example with the middle and index finger simultaneously. Place them on the string before plucking and pull outwards to sound the notes. Some players like Brent Mason use acrylic nails to give these notes a pick-like attack, but, personally speaking, I just use the flesh of the fingers. Both options are fine.

Example 4a:

Now add the pick. Here's a short example based around an E Major chord. The first note is plucked with the pick then the *double stop* is played with the fingers. Simply alternate between the two.

As an experiment, try playing this idea with just the pick. While it is possible, it's a lot more work and doesn't sound the same at all.

Example 4b:

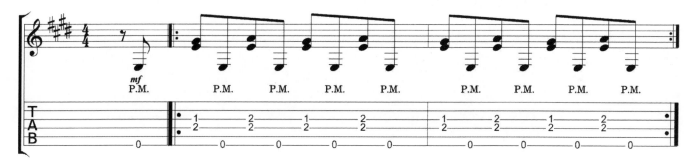

Next it's important to practice the 'pinch', which is when you use the pick and fingers together.

Example 4c:

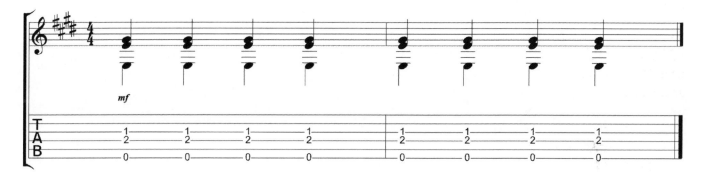

Before adding syncopation, it's important to get used to the pick alternating between the sixth and fourth strings. This example teaches that idea by playing the bass notes with down-strokes.

Example 4d:

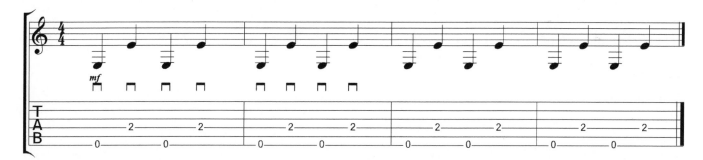

As with the previous example, the pick continues to play on all 4 beats. The pinch only occurs on beats 2 and 4. The pick still plays the low notes. The notation uses downward facing stems for notes played with the pick and upward facing stems for notes played with the fingers.

Example 4e:

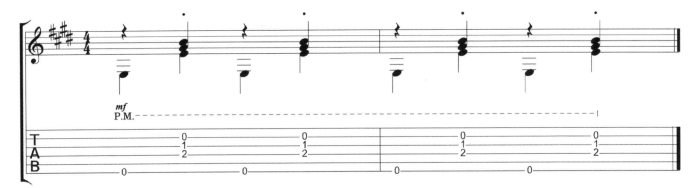

The next example expands on the previous idea by adding syncopation. The second double stop is pulled forward by an 1/8th note to create an accented offbeat. This is a big part of the rockabilly style, though the Travis picking country fingerstyle subject will be covered much more deeply in book two.

Example 4f:

Here's an example that requires you to double-pick the double stops to create an interesting rhythmic pattern consisting of two groups of three, followed by one group of two. Although the bar contains eight notes, the traditional backbeat has now been removed. Instead of accenting the 2 and 4, count "1 2 3 1 2 3 1 2" and accent the 1s to give you a better idea of the feel.

Example 4g:

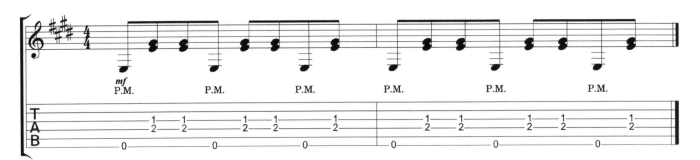

The next example is similar to the rhythm playing you'll to hear in Merle Haggard's band. Based around an E7 chord, use the pick for the notes on the low E string, and the fingers for the double stops. This example requires tight time keeping skills in the fretting hand as you're required to pluck open strings and hammer onto a fretted note. Use the 1st finger for the hammered note, then fret both notes on the 2nd fret with a 2nd finger barre.

Example 4h:

Example 4h embellishes the previous riff to cover four bars. In the second measure you'll need to play the high E string and let all the strings ring. As with the double stops, use a picking hand finger to sound this note. In the final measure the same idea is played, but this time ends with an alternate-picked idea on the D and A strings.

Example 4i:

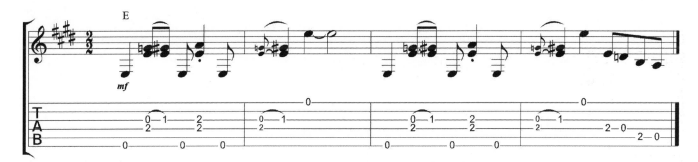

The next example draws influence from Boogie-Woogie bands by using a solid stream of 1/8th notes. In order to execute the double-stroke with the pick it is easiest to play an up-stroke followed by a down (as indicated above the tablature). Ideas like this are as at home in the blues as they are in country music.

Example 4j:

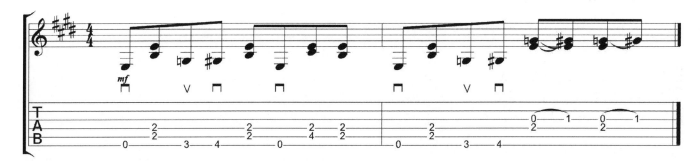

Here is an idea similar to example 4g, but this time in the key of A. In the second bar there's a little melodic trick in the double stop that takes an A5 chord and moves the lowest note down from the 5th to the b5th to the 4th. Not only does this give a pleasing bluesy edge, but it opens up some sonic options when riffing.

Example 4k:

The next example expands on the previous idea by adding more single notes while leaving the double stops as accents in the rhythm. While there are notes here that could be seen as part of a scale, they're more about linking chord tones together than a scale in their own right. We will look at scales later!

Example 4l:

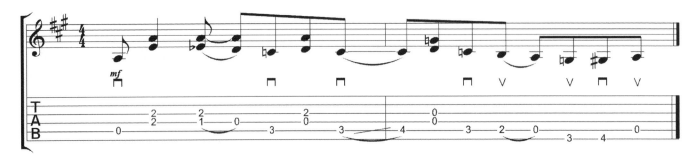

Here's an example that uses the low open E and finger-picked double stops as a starting point, but adds a walk-up for melodic interest in the bass. Use the pick for the single notes and fingers for the double-stops.

Example 4m:

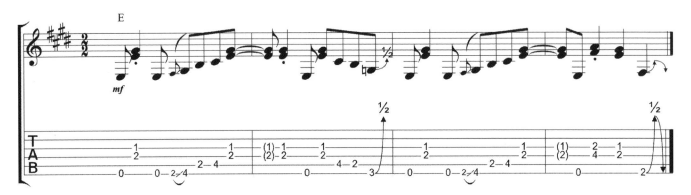

The next example applies the hybrid picking concept to a chord progression to give you a better idea of how someone like Brad Paisley would use it in a song. Played in the key of E, this I, V, vi, IV progression is outlined with simple chord-patterns, so don't lose sight of the original barre chord when adding the single notes.

Example 4n:

The final example in this chapter uses hybrid picked *riffing* to a chord progression in the key of G. The G Major chord is played in open position while the C Major and D7 use barre chords in higher positions.

Example 4o:

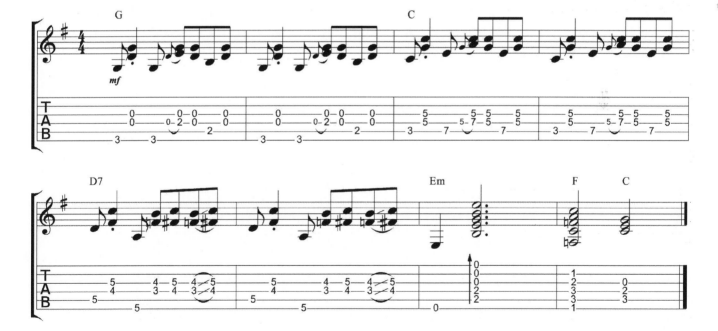

Hopefully, you can see that in Country music, chords are thought of as *individual events* and are embellished as such. Rather than playing the scale of G Major over a whole progression in G, the thought process is much closer to jazz, where each individual chord is treated and embellished as an entity in its own right.

Part Two: Scales, Arpeggios and Lead Guitar

In Part Two, you'll develop a full range of scales, arpeggios and soloing approaches that can be applied to of country music.

In this section, you'll learn:

- Scale theory
- Open position scales
- Movable scales
- The CAGED system
- Soloing with intervals
- Relationships between chords, arpeggios and scales
- How to use patterns to make real music
- Arpeggio concepts
- Soloing ideas

Mastering the skills in this section will free your mind from thinking too much about the neck when playing, as well as preparing your fingers for the more technically demanding aspects of country guitar like banjo rolls and open string ideas.

Don't rush through these ideas, take your time and don't be afraid to jump back to earlier chapters to review concepts, techniques, and theory. Listen to country music as much as possible and try to recognise the techniques in everything you hear.

Chapter Five: Country Scale Primer

In order to develop your knowledge of chords, harmony, and soloing, it's important to get to grips with the sounds and common fingerings of a selection of country music scales.

This chapter will build your knowledge of intervals and create proficiency in:

- The Minor Pentatonic scale
- The Blues scale
- The Major Pentatonic scale
- The "Country" scale
- Open position fingerings
- Movable forms
- Parallel vs derivative modal theory

Coming from the Greek penta, - meaning "five", and tonic, - meaning "based on the key note", a Pentatonic scale is any scale that consists of five notes.

The Minor Pentatonic scale is the workhorse of countless respectable country, blues, rock, metal, and even jazz players; many of the greatest of all time use it exclusively, never feeling the need to look elsewhere to create genre-defining signature sounds, so it would be foolish to overlook it!

Example 5a shows the E Minor Pentatonic scale played in the open position. At this stage, don't worry too much about picking technique or theory, just concentrate on hearing the sound of the scale.

Example 5a:

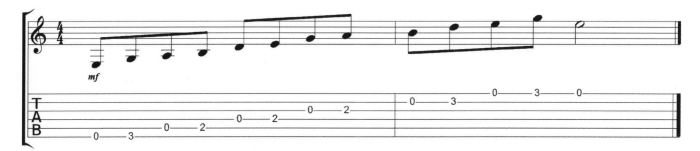

As previously stated, much can be achieved with this scale, including moving the entire form up or down the neck to suit any key. For example, here's the same scale shifted up the neck three frets to give you the G Minor Pentatonic scale. Note that the root note is found on the low E string, and is played with the 1st finger.

Example 5b:

Looking at this scale on a diagram gives you the chance to see the intervals at play. Intervals are what gives the scale it's character. Consisting of the Root, b3, 4, 5 and b7, the scale contains the same notes as a Minor 7 chord (R, b3, 5, b7) but with an added 4th.

G Minor Pentatonic
scale

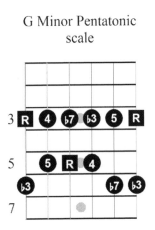

One might surmise that this means the G Minor Pentatonic scale will work exclusively over Minor chords, but the truth is a little surprising. In fact, while the Minor 3rd of a G Minor Pentatonic scale should clash horribly with the Major 3rd of a G Major or G7 chord, the result is pleasing tension best described as "bluesy" or "gritty".

Example 5c demonstrates the G Minor Pentatonic played against a G Minor chord vamp. It sounds like a good fit, capturing the quality of the chord in a pleasing way.

Example 5c:

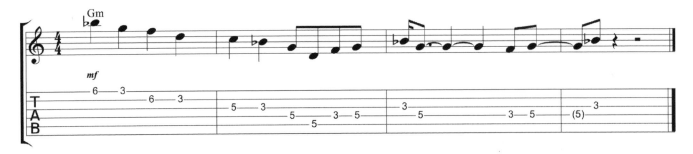

The next example uses a different G Minor Pentatonic lick against a G *Major* chord to see how it sounds.

You'll notice that I'm bending those b3rds (Bbs) a little sharp to create a bluesy quality, this is known as a "blues curl" and doesn't *quite* raise the note from Bb to B, but hints at something in between.

Example 5d:

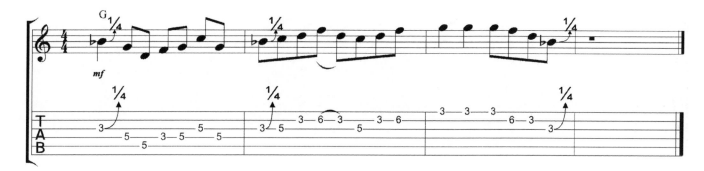

When getting to grips with scales on the guitar, it is important to understand that your ear must match your technical proficiency, if not surpass it. You must practice all your ideas and exercises in some sort of harmonic context so you're not just learning how to play the lick, but you're also building a *relationship* with it in context, and internalising how it makes you feel.

To create an instant backing track, I use a looper pedal by TC electronic when practicing. This repeats a chord indefinitely so that I never lose the harmonic context; there are numerous options when it comes to recording backing tracks, but this feels the quickest and best-sounding to me.

While it is important to learn scales that cover the entire neck, at this stage there's more benefit to be had from building control of a scale in one area before introducing multiple fingerings and position shifts. That said, it's also useful to have little "bolt-on" notes that can be added to the top or bottom of a pattern to extend your vocabulary.

For example, below is the G Minor Pentatonic scale from the previous example, this time with a little additional range at the top and at the bottom. This will come in handy quite soon.

Extended G Minor Pentatonic scale

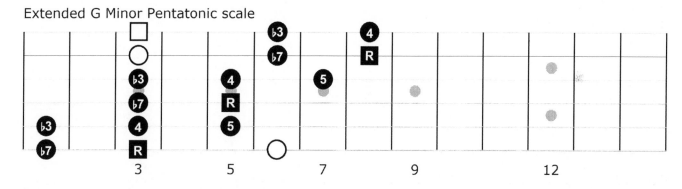

You'll notice that some of the notes are hollow, this is to help outline a "roadmap" used to move up the neck. The white notes are possible fingerings of the scale notes, but re-fingered in the following example to create an easier line.

In order to play the three consecutive notes on the A string, use the 1st finger on the 1st fret, the 3rd finger on the 3rd fret, and then shift with the 3rd finger to play the 5th fret.

Example 5e:

The following lick is an example of how common this bolt-on approach is: I opt to slide to the 5th fret on the G string rather than picking the same note on the B string. Not only is this easier, but the articulation is different. The slide adds something to the lick and is a big part of why it sounds the way it does.

Example 5f:

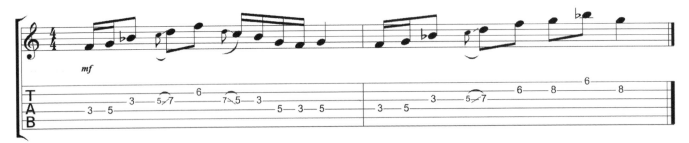

This final Minor Pentatonic example uses the previous position shift idea, but this time played back in the open position. Here, the scale is used to create a fill between the backbeat on the E Major chord in a way that is typical of the style.

Example 5g:

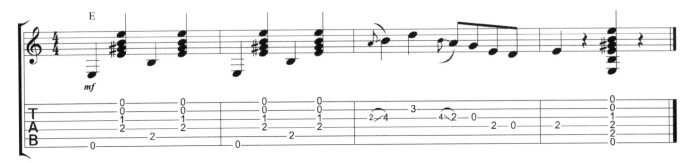

The next scale *could* be called a *hexatonic*, meaning that it contains six notes. However, looking at the following diagram, you'll notice that it's the same shape as the earlier Minor Pentatonic scale but with one added note. Throughout my years of teaching, I'm yet to meet anyone that thinks of this as a new scale as it's so obviously a Minor Pentatonic scale with an added extra note. The extra note is a b5 interval (often called the *blues note*).

G Blues scale

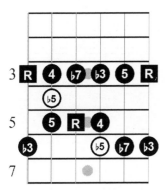

This b5 has a very distinctive sound, and is normally used as an interesting passing note but can be played as a dark note to pause on. Learn how this note sounds until it's something you're able to add to your playing as and when you hear it.

Example 5h:

The "problem" with the above scales is that while they're usable in country music, they tend to add a blues influence to the country vocabulary, creating a sad, minor vibe. When you listen to timeless country music, a large portion of it is in Major keys, so being able to play a Major sound is essential to the genre.

The first port of call for any serious country player is the Major Pentatonic scale, the Minor Pentatonic's Major, yet soulful, cousin. The intervals in the G Major, and G Minor Pentatonic scales are compared below:

G Major Pentatonic   G Minor Pentatonic
scale   scale

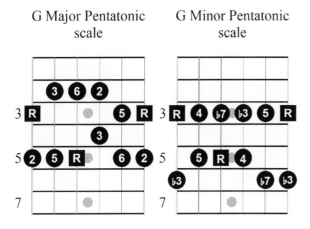

When compared to the Minor Pentatonic, there's clearly a different set of intervals at play in the Major Pentatonic scale. While the Minor Pentatonic scale contains R, b3rd, 4th, 5th, and b7th, the Major Pentatonic drops the darker b3rd, 4th, and b7th in favour of the sweeter sounding 2nd, 3rd and 6th giving a formula of 1, 2, 3, 5, 6.

I find it helpful associate a chord sound to every scale, so that when someone asks, "what does the Major Pentatonic scale sound like?", I'm simply able to play a chord that instantly creates the correct vibe of the scale. Remember, chords come from scales, and a chord is nothing more than certain notes of a scale played at the same time.

With the G Minor Pentatonic scale, the R, 3rd, 5th, and 7th gives you R, b3, 5, b7 - or a Minor 7 chord.

Example 5i:

Using the intervals of the Major Pentatonic scale, the R, 3rd, 5th and 6th create a G6 chord.

Example 5j:

One trick often used by guitar players is to use the Minor Pentatonic scale shape to play the Major Pentatonic scale.

It is easy to use the Minor Pentatonic scale shape you already know to form a Major Pentatonic scale with the same root note. Simply move the Minor Pentatonic scale down three frets. Your little finger should now be on the root where your first finger was originally.

For example, Play the C Minor Pentatonic scale by placing your first finger on the 8th fret of the low E string. Then, move the whole shape down three frets so your 4th finger is now on the 8th fret. Play the notes of the Minor Pentatonic scale shape beginning and ending with your little finger on the 8th fret. You are now playing a C Major Pentatonic scale. Play this over a C Major chord vamp to hear the effect.

Example 5k:

Here's a classic country lick using this pattern. Note the use of the Eb to approach the E; this movement is very common in this style.

Example 5l:

We can use the Blues scale too, and apply it to the Major and Minor relationship. Playing the Blues scale shape as a Major Pentatonic idea is very common and is referred to as the *Country* scale.

C Country scale

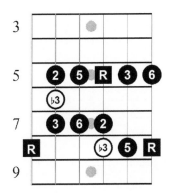

This isn't an all-encompassing scale that will turn anyone into a country-picking master, but the combination of that sweet Major Pentatonic tonality, along with the added bluesy b3, creates a unique sound heard in most country guitar solos.

As with the b5 in the Blues scale, the b3 in the Country scale is a tension note which should be handled carefully, its most common use is as a chromatic approach note to the natural 3rd, as shown in the following lick.

Example 5m:

Another common approach to country music soloing is to use a Major scale over a full chord progression in one key. For example, the Major scale will work over any chord in the key of the G Major, so for chord progressions like G / Em / C / D7, you can treat all four chords as coming from the G Major scale. Let's take a look at some of those major scales and learn some licks.

Here are the most important Major scales in the played in the open position. These are a big part of the country music style.

Play the notated chord first to get the sound of the key in your ear, then play the scale slowly enough to really *hear* what you're playing. Try to hear each note before you play it, as not only does this help develop your ear, but also puts you in a position of *reactive* improvisation.

First up is an open C Major scale

Example 5n:

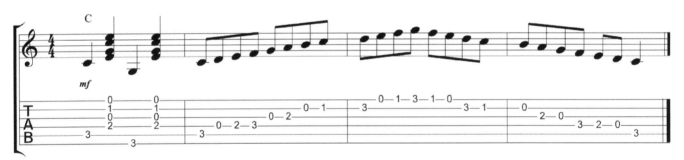

Here's a lick typical among bluegrass players. It sticks closely to the scale, aside from the added b3 (Eb) towards the end of the lick.

Example 5o:

Next is a G Major scale (G, A, B, C, D, E, F#). When you play this scale, pay attention to the location of the new note (F#). Not only will this help you to see the difference between scales, but it will also help you start learning where notes are on the neck.

Example 5p:

Here's a great little country melody using that scale.

Example 5q:

And one more lick that's a little more challenging.

Example 5r:

Next is a D Major scale, which introduces the note C# (D, E, F#, G, A, B, C#).

Example 5s:

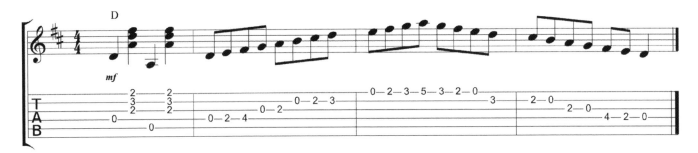

Here's a lick using that scale. As with previous examples, the b3 (F) has been used to make it sound a little more country.

Example 5t:

The A Major scale adds a G# to the mix (A, B, C#, D, E, F#, G#).

Example 5u:

This lick in A Major shows that as you add more accidentals, these licks can become a little trickier to play.

Example 5v:

One last open scale to learn is E Major, which introduces a D# (E, F#, G#, A, B, C#, D#).

Example 5w:

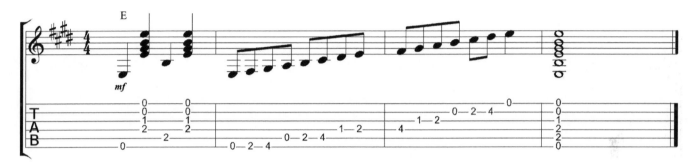

Here's a lick you'll see in one of the later solos. Notice how notes that are a tone apart are connected with chromatic passing tones. This isn't something that needs to be analysed in great detail; it fits nicely under the fingers and sounds great.

Example 5x:

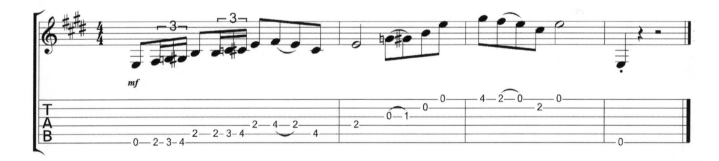

The next example it a typical bluegrass-style solo line using the G Major scale to give an idea of how incredible pickers like Tony Rice or Doc Watson use open positions.

The trickiest part of this style is the discipline of playing open-string notes with equal rhythmic values to the fretted notes. Many players use the fretting hand to keep the picking hand in check; a finger goes down - you pick a note. However, when we introduce open string notes, this automation can get lost. Take your time and make sure you're comfortable combining open strings and fretted notes evenly in these scales, as this technique will become very important later on.

Example 5y:

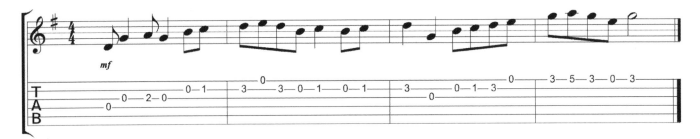

Here's another bluegrass type melody, this time in the key of D Major.

Example 5z:

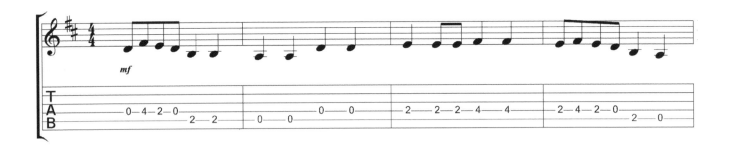

The obvious challenge with the five 'open' scales studied so far is that they're all fingered differently. However, it is possible to use a movable form (just like a barre chord) to play any scale, no matter which key you're in.

Using the Major Pentatonic scale as a starting point, let's fill in the other notes needed to create a movable Major scale.

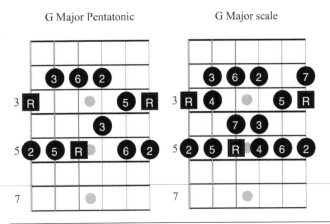

While this isn't the only movable form, it's a good starting point when soloing in a Major key.

The following example demonstrates one country lick played in four different keys ,by simply moving the shape up and down the neck. In comparison to developing vocabulary using open position scales, this should feel easy, all while opening up the fretboard.

Example 5z1:

Each example so far has been played over major chords. While major chords absolutely occur in country music, it's often more common to find progressions built from Dominant chords.

A Dominant 7 chord consists of a Major chord with an added b7th degree. The "correct" scale to play over a Dominant 7 chord is often called the "Mixolydian mode", but in country music, the Mixolydian mode is normally just called the Dominant 7 scale, or viewed as a major scale with a b7.

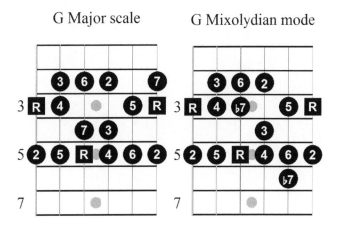

G Major scale   G Mixolydian mode

I'll often think of the 'G Mixolydian' scale as the 'G7' scale, because it's the scale that fits over a G7 chord. It contains the intervals of that chord and is my first choice for creating melodic ideas.

The following example showcases the sound of the Dominant 7 scale to closely outline the G7 harmony. Note the use of Bb as an approach to the 3rd of G7 (B).

Example 5z2:

Here's another lick using that scale.

Example 5z3:

The ultimate goal is to start seeing all available notes as simply sounds at your disposal. There are twelve notes, and each one has its own unique sound over different chords. While it's common to pool sets of notes that sound great together as 'scales', the other notes aren't unplayable, they're just acquired sounds that take time to master. It's also O.K. to mix and match scales to get the sound you want.

There are many more scales, modes, and arpeggios to learn, but musicians don't build knowledge by simply knowing music theory. The most important knowledge is acquired through musical experience, so the next step is to get a feel for traditional country licks and vocabulary, and learn how many country players see this language on the guitar neck.

Chapter Six: CAGED Positions

One of the most rewarding aspects of country guitar is how harmonically aware the genre will make you, and also learning to navigate the entirety of the neck is a big part of the sound of everyone from Albert Lee to Johnny Hiland.

The most common guitar neck visualization method is to see licks and phrases as embellishments to small chord forms. This technique goes right back to the '20s and is nothing more than common sense: Each small chord form is a three-note fragment (triad) that is used as a harmonic anchor. It is then easy to decorate this anchor with melodies without ever losing the sound of the chord.

Over time, this anchor approach has expanded into a full system of visualization, which is taught at institutions the world over due to the importance it places on harmony. It is a perfect way to think when playing blues, jazz, and country music. This 'CAGED' system is really nothing more than the result of the natural geometry of the neck. Despite being named The CAGED system, the approach actually completely 'uncages' you, allowing you to play freely anywhere on the guitar neck.

So far you've looked at a selection of scales that began with the root note on the low E string. This amounts to 1/5th of the system. This is a pretty sizable chunk, but let's move back a step and look at how that scale fits into the CAGED system.

The CAGED system begins by looking at the five C, A, G, E, and D open-position chords.

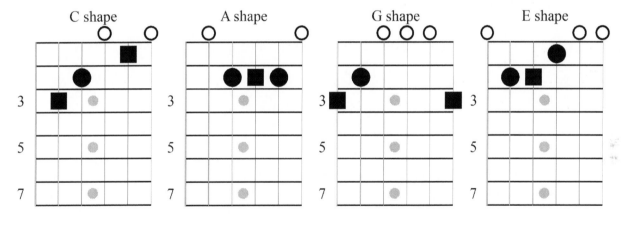

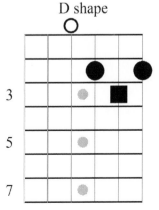

I break each chord down into one of two categories; chords where the notes are 'behind' the root note, and chords where the notes are 'in front of' the root note.

For example, on the C Major chord, the root is played with the 3rd finger. The other notes in the chord are *behind* this note as they're on lower frets (closer to the nut of the guitar). The same is true of the G Major chord.

In the A Major chord, the root is on the open A string, and the other notes of the chord are *in front* (on higher frets) of that note. The E Major and D Major chords both fit into this category.

Each of these CAGED chord shapes can be played as a barre, and therefore moved anywhere on the neck. For example, moving the 'C Shape' up in semitones allows us to play the chords of C# Major, then D Major, The D# Major, etc.

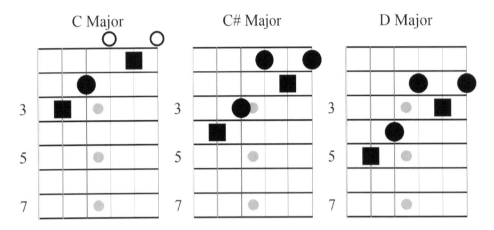

Using each of the CAGED shapes (and with a little awareness of where the root notes are located on the fretboard), we can now play *any* chord in five different places on the guitar neck.

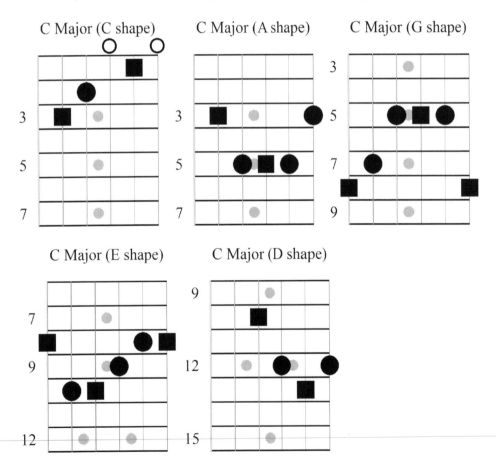

Some of these shapes share the same root location (for example, the 'A' and 'C' shapes of C Major both have a root on the 3rd fret). This is where the idea of 'forward' and 'backward' shapes is important. Try not to have too much bias towards one shape otherwise you might find develop some grey areas in your fretboard knowledge. It's ok to feel stronger in some positions than others, but you don't want any blank spots on the neck.

The next example demonstrates how these small harmonic fragments (triads) fall on the neck, and how they relate to the CAGED chords. Each three-note grouping contains the adjacent notes C, E, and G.

Measure 1 falls around the A shape of the CAGED system.

Measure 2 falls around the E shape, and measure 3 falls around the C shape.

You'll soon notice that a huge amount of country guitar is built around these basic chord forms.

Example 6a:

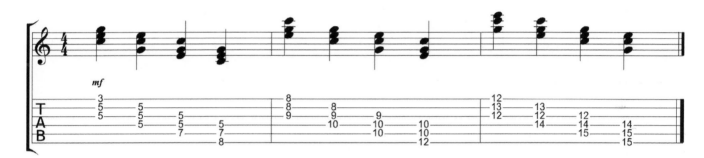

These triads can be used to play interesting chord ideas around any chord progression:

Example 6b:

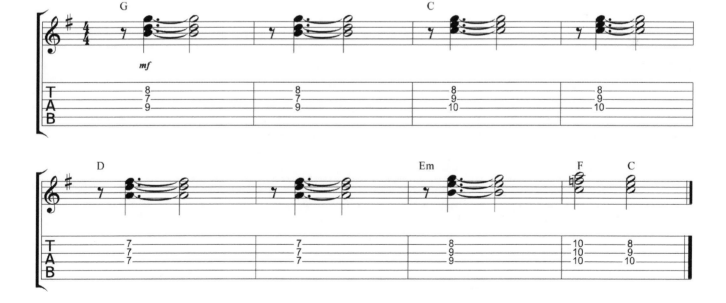

Here's the same triad roadmap, but outlined melodically. The great thing is that this approach doesn't sound at all like playing scales; for the most part you're playing the notes of the triad but embellishing them with notes a semitone below. This is how early country players approached soloing as it results in solos with a strong sense of harmony

Example 6c:

This is also my approach when I solo. Even when I play a lot of notes, all I'm normally doing is decorating small three- or four-string chord voicings that I visualise on the neck.

To see how this approach is applied in country music, I've written an example over an A7 vamp. Check out the following three diagrams which show an A triad and a G triad (three notes found in the A Mixolydian scale).

The triads are shown as black notes, while the other notes of the A7 chord (which I use for melody) are hollow.

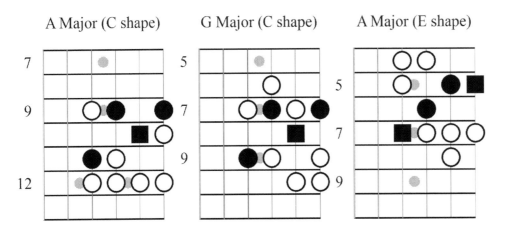

Let's use this roadmap to navigate from the 9th fret area down to the 5th fret in an interesting and harmonically strong way. This lick doesn't sound like running up and down scales but instead creates something exciting and unpredictable.

Example 6d:

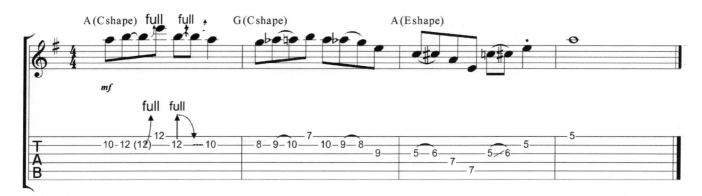

Here's another lick using the same roadmap. This one is a little more challenging to play and demonstrates that it's possible to interpret CAGED positions in a variety of ways.

The lick begins by approaching the 3rd from a semitone below and ascends the scale before playing two notes from A7 the chord as a double stop. In measure two, the double stop moves down to target two notes from the G Major chord and create a nice G/A sound, before shifting down to the E shape at the 5th fret with a typical country lick to finish.

Example 6e:

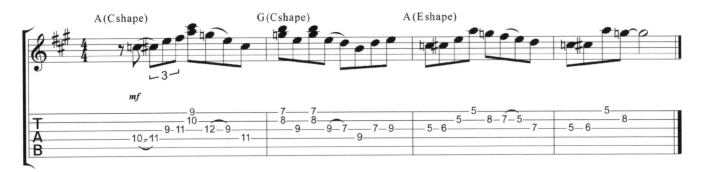

Building the connection between chords and scale patterns is essential when navigating the neck fluently, so take time to work through each of the following diagrams carefully. First find the root note of the chord (shown as a black square), then the chord should light up in your mind (black notes in the diagrams), before finally adding the notes of the scale around it (indicated by hollow notes).

First up is the C shape. In black, you'll see the notes of the chord. Around this, you have the notes needed to pad the chord out to become a scale.

E7 (C shape)

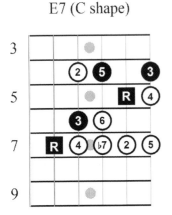

The following is an E7 lick played in the C shape. As usual the b3rd is used as an approach note to the 3rd of the chord.

Example 6f:

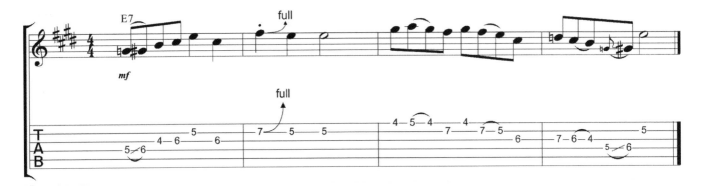

Here's another lick in that position.

Example 6g:

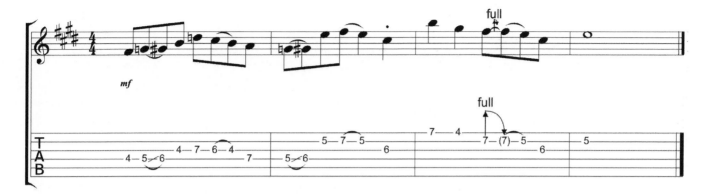

Next up is E Major played with the A shape. The root can be found on the A string and is played with either the 1st finger (for the chord) or the 2nd finger (for the scale).

E7 (A shape)

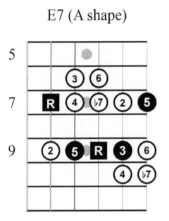

And here's a lick in that position to give you an idea of how this area can be used.

Example 6h:

Here's another lick based around the A shape, this time using some double stops that fit nicely under the fingers.

Example 6i:

The G shape is often overlooked but contains many great opportunities for melodies.

E7 (G shape)

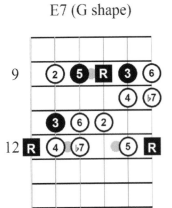

This lick uses a classic pedal steel style bend and some Country scale ideas.

Example 6j:

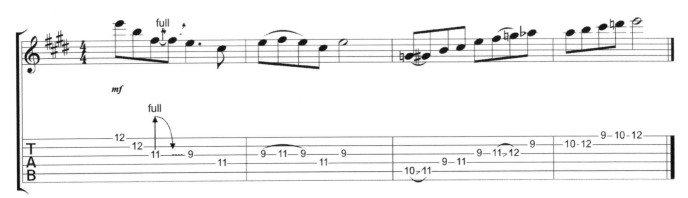

Here's a second lick in that position to demonstrate the endless possibilities found in each area of the neck.

Example 6k:

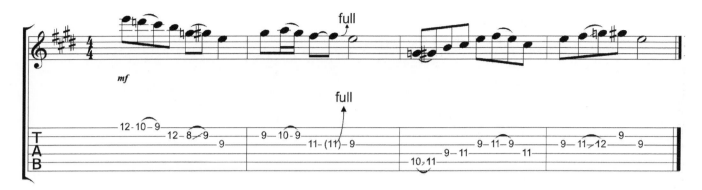

The E shape is the most common position. In fact, it was covered in the previous chapter. It's included here for completion.

E7 (E shape)

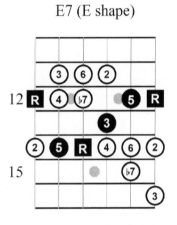

Here's another lick in this position to expand your vocabulary further.

Example 6l:

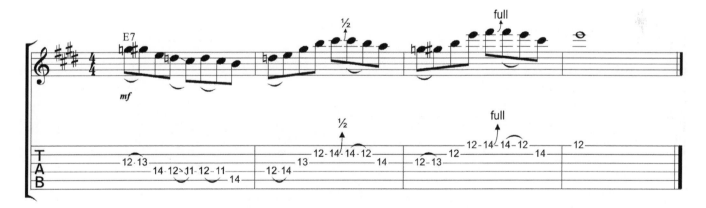

And one more idea here, this time using a few more chromatic passing notes to connect notes of the scale.

Example 6m:

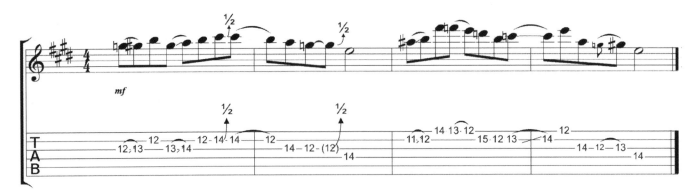

Finally, here's the D shape.

E7 (D shape)

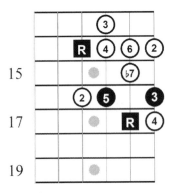

I find this shape a little harder to use when soloing. I do use it, but usually while moving up to the C shape, or down to the E. Here's an idea that stays in position.

Example 6n:

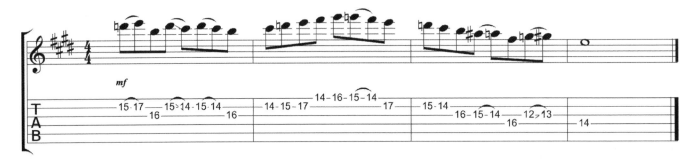

Here's an example that links multiple positions of the E Major scale together. Pay attention to the markings above the tab to see where the CAGED point of reference changes.

Example 6o:

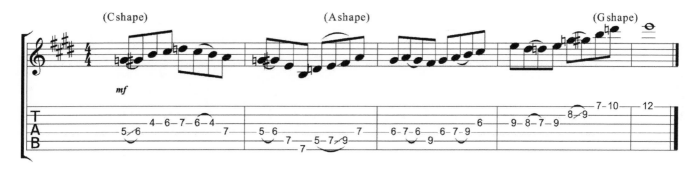

Here's one final E Major idea that stars up high on the neck and moves downward in a manner that conjures up images of Nashville ace, Brent Mason.

Example 6p:

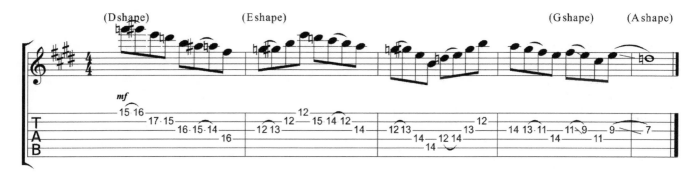

Now to draw this all together, here's an example of some of this vocabulary being used over the chord changes of G7 - A7 - D7 - G7.

Over the G7 chord, we play the lick found in example 6p, but here it is moved down the neck to fit a G7 chord rather than the E7 looked at previously.

To hit the A7 chord, move up the neck by two frets and play within the E shape again, moving to the A shape to switch to the D7 chord with a lick reminiscent to example 6h. This then resolves down to the E shape, targeting the 3rd of G7 (B).

Example 6q:

Here's another example over those same chord changes.

This time you begin in the A shape with a lick similar to example 6h, but moved up to a G7 chord. As you're in the 10th fret area, changing to the A7 chord is as easy as moving to the C shape, which is targeted by landing on the 5th of the chord (E).

It's possible to stay in this area of the neck for the D7 chord by switching to the E shape (played at the 10th fret), and to hit the G7 I've moved down the neck by playing the C shape over the G7, targeting the 3rd (B).

Example 6r:

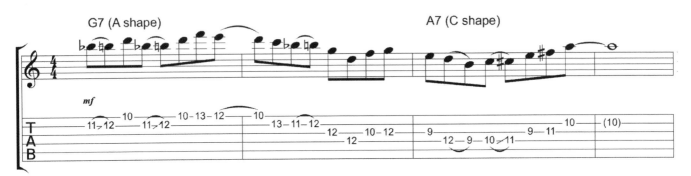

Being aware of the little chord forms as you move around the neck will help your licks feel musical, rather than just running up and down scales because they automatically place emphasis on chord tones. This approach takes a while to master, but once these frameworks are opened up, you'll be connecting the whole neck in no time at all.

Chapter Seven - 3rds & 6ths Interval Licks

Country guitar playing is heavily influenced by other instruments, and none are more notable than the double stop ideas found on the fiddle or lap/pedal steel guitar.

Not only will these intervallic ideas give you an authentic country sound, they will open up your ears to new ideas and also encourage you to move away from just playing scales up and down.

Playing diatonic 3rds consists of taking a note, and then playing a note a 3rd higher in the scale. For example, In C Major, (C D E F G A B) a 3rd above C is E, a 3rd above D is F, and so on.

Playing intervals alone won't instantly give you country sound though. The following example consists of diatonic 3rds within the G Major scale, but this has a more mechanical, 'neoclassical' sound that you'd expect from a player like Paul Gilbert.

Example 7a:

You'll notice that some intervals are on the same strings and some are on adjacent strings. Playing intervals on different strings has two benefits. Firstly, the notes are able to ring into each other if that's the desired sound, and secondly, you are able to play up and down the neck on string pairs instead of across the neck in a scale shape.

Here's an example using diatonic 3rds in the G Mixolydian scale to outline a G7 chord. The pattern consists of playing the lower note of the pair, the higher note, repeating the lower note and sliding up to the next interval.

Example 7b:

When doing this, it's very useful to be able to see the bigger chord forms as a point of reference. This gives you a route into the interval and a way to resolve it.

Below are 3rds of G Mixolydian on the G and B strings, visualized around the E, C and A barre forms. Note that the chord grips are shown as hollow notes, with the notes of the 3rd-pairs given in black and connected with lines.

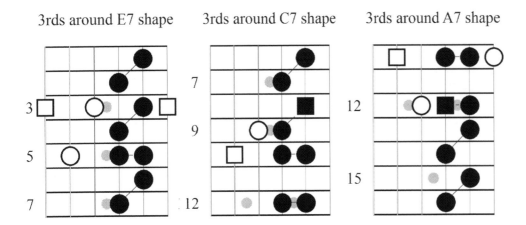

Here is a lick that uses these 3rds as a way to get from the E shape at the 3rd fret to the A shape at the 10th fret.

The lick in measure one is lick similar to an idea played many times in this book; a hybrid of the pentatonic scale and the G7 chord, using both the Minor and Major 3rd. Measure two slides up the neck using 3rds and resolves to the A shape.

Example 7c:

A clearer framework for this type of idea might be to see it on the neck rather than as a lick. It's not important how you get from point A to point B, just focus on the concept.

3rds Around G7 CAGED Shapes

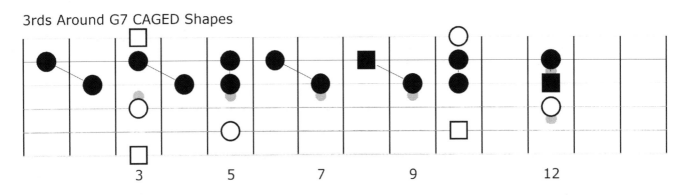

Another way to use these 3rds is as extensions to melodic fragments you're already familiar with. The following lick sits around an E shape and uses notes which are already familiar. To develop the idea a little more I've added the 3rd interval below the chord shape.

Example 7d:

A similar approach can be applied to any position. Playing 3rds with the C chord as a framework might result in the following idea. As with many licks, combining the Minor and Major 3rds is an essential part of the sound.

Example 7e:

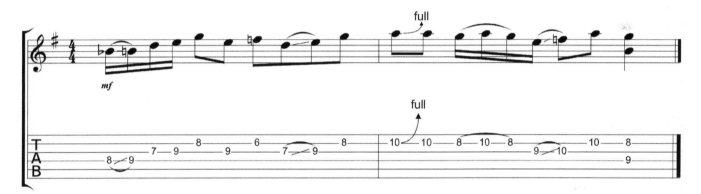

One of the exciting options presented by 3rds is the possibility of connecting two shapes together with chromatic passing notes. These work great when playing rhythm guitar as shown in the following pedal steel-inspired example.

Example 7f:

Here's another chordal example, this time moving down from the E shape of a G7 chord to give an ending that would fit well on a swing tune.

Example 7g:

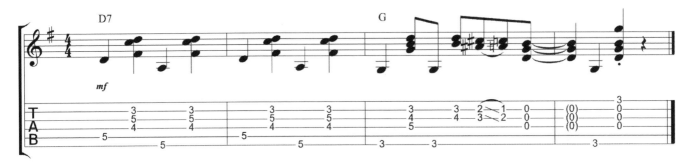

It's worth considering that like these aren't just limited to the G and B string, as this example on the B and E string shows.

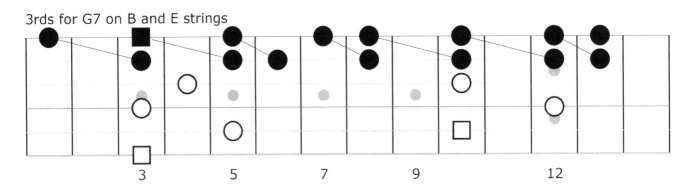

3rds for G7 on B and E strings

Example 7h:

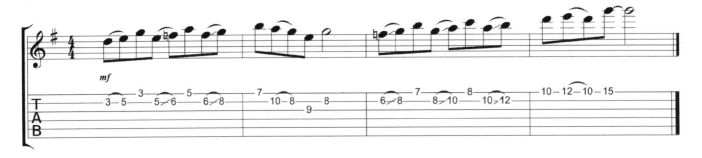

Here's an example on the D and G strings. This would be a great way to play some modern country rhythm guitar on a slow ballad.

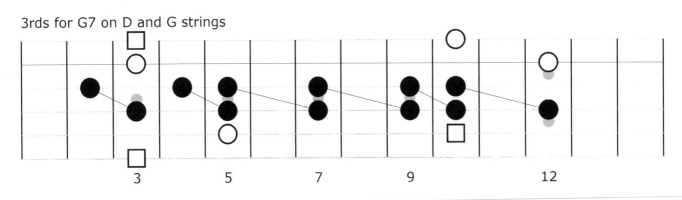

3rds for G7 on D and G strings

Example 7i:

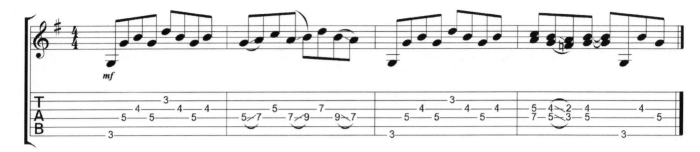

3rds are often thought of as being 'sweet' sounding when used melodically, but their close cousin, the 6th, has just as much sweetness to it's sound.

The interval of C to E is a 3rd; but if you *invert* that interval and go from E to C, you create a 6th (E F G A B C). 3rds and 6ths are very closely related, despite each having their own unique sound.

The following example demonstrates how a classical guitarist might play diatonic 6ths in the key of G. They sound nice, but they're very tricky to play like this.

Example 7j:

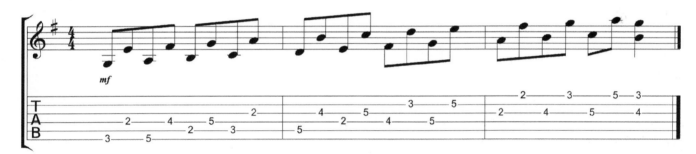

An easier (and more practical) way to play 6ths is on string pairs, like the G and high E shown below in the key of G.

Example 7k:

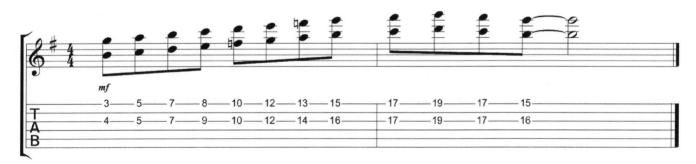

6ths with chromatic passing notes over G7

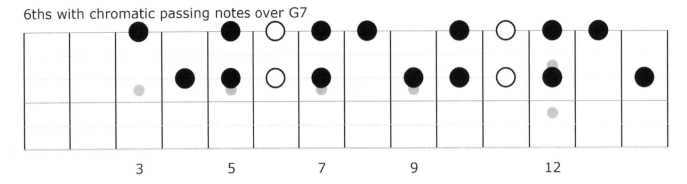

Here's the same basic idea, but this time I've linked the parallel shapes with chromatic passing notes. The non-diatonic (chromatic) 6ths have been marked in brackets. They sound great as passing notes, but you wouldn't want to sit on them on a strong beat of the bar!

Example 7l:

Here's an example of how these 6ths can be used when soloing and creating melodies. Beginning with the G Major Pentatonic scale, the lick quickly moves up to the 7th fret and descends down in 6ths, ending on the 3rd (B).

Example 7m:

Next up is an example that uses chromatic passing notes between 6th intervals. The lick begins with a bluegrass cliché before moving up the neck and playing 6ths around the E and C shapes.

Example 7n:

As with the 3rds, you may find these concepts easier to see on the fretboard rather than as a lick.

6ths around E7 shape   6ths around C7 shape

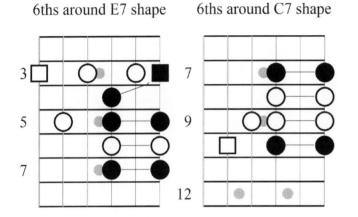

Again, these ideas aren't limited to just one string set, and should be explored on the D and B, A and G, and E and D sets.

6ths with chromatic passing notes over G7

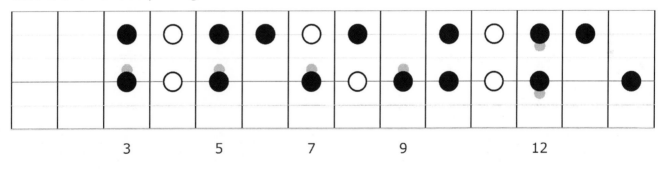

Here's an example on A7 that features 6ths on the A and G strings. The lick begins in the open A shape and moves up to the E shape. The second half of the lick jumps to the G and E strings for an ending similar previous ideas.

Example 7o:

Another common way to embellish these 6th ideas is with this *chicken pickin'* idea. The lowest note of each 6th is approached chromatically from a tone below before the higher note is plucked aggressively with a picking-hand finger. Early country players would often play all three notes by sliding the third finger. It's certainly not as accurate as using one finger per fret, but it's full of attitude.

Example 7p:

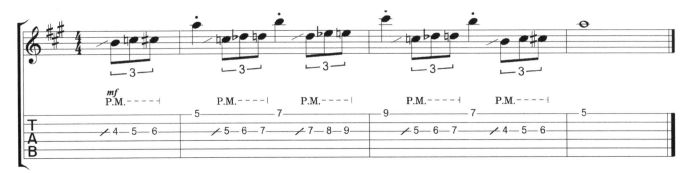

Here's a similar example but this time descending the neck and resolving with a typical pedal steel imitation bend.

Licks like this are very common in the playing of greats like Roy Nichols.

Example 7q:

Here's a final, more advanced lick in A that features 3rds and some sliding 6ths.

Example 7r:

While 3rds and 6ths aren't the only intervals you'll find in the playing of country guitar icons, they're certainly the most common and idiomatic.

Chapter Eight - String Bending Skills

One of the most common tools in the arsenal of the country guitarist is the bend, and it is one of the more unique effects available on stringed instruments like the guitar.

The electric guitar draws influence and inspiration from fiddle, as well as steel guitar players. One of the best ways to get to grips with country vocabulary is to listen to other instruments and adapt their ideas to your own instrument.

Developed from the lap steel guitar, the pedal steel was developed in the '40s to give players more musical options. The lap steel guitar is an instrument with ten strings tuned to an open chord (normally E9), and played with a large metal bar (known as a tone bar). This felt quite limiting to many players, so engineers started creating complex mechanical systems that could change the pitch of a string via the use of a pedal. Over time this would result in a common set up of three foot pedals, and four knee levers that all raised or lowered the pitch of different strings.

These pedals allowed players to play a chord and then change the pitch of one or more of those notes while others stayed static. This is an iconic sound, integral to the sound of country music, so give it the attention it deserves by listening and mimicking its unique character when you can.

Notable steel players include, Speedy West, Buddy Emmons, Paul Franklin, and Randle Currie to name just a few.

One of the biggest differences you'll find among country guitar players vs blues or rock players, is that in country there is great importance placed on the note you're bending *to*, rather than just bending to create a musical effect.

The other big difference between bent notes in country and bent notes in other genres, is that in country you'll often bend one note *while* sustaining others. In order to execute these bends, the force must come from the finger rather than the wrist. Remember that you're imitating a pedal steel guitar, so you want the bend to sound as mechanical as possible. Don't take your time! - Bend straight up to the note as though it were done with a mechanical pedal.

The first pedal steel example is in the key of A Major and takes the notes B, and E, and bends the B (the 9th) up a tone to C# (3rd) to create an A Major triad. In order to execute this bend, fix the 3rd finger on the 5th fret, while the 1st and 2nd finger rest on the 4th fret and work together to support the bend.

Example 8a:

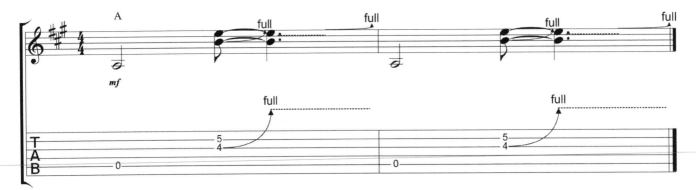

The previous example can be expanded by adding the root (A) on the high E string.

When looking at these diagrams, the notes played are black, while the notes of the chord are hollow. This allows you to see the notes you're playing, and where each bend targets.

Steel Bend 2-3

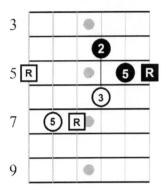

Example 8b:

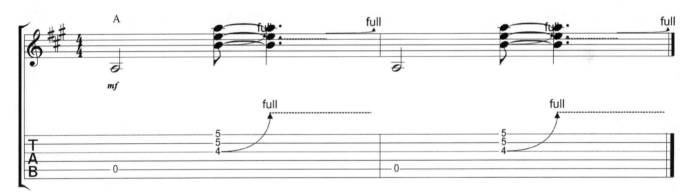

The next example jumps up the neck to bend the 9th (B) up to the 3rd (C#), while holding the 5th (E) on the high E string. This fits into the A shape of the CAGED system.

Steel Bend 2-3

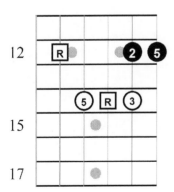

Example 8c:

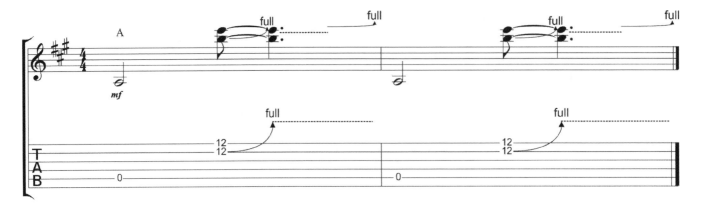

Here, this bending idea is used in a lick that descends the neck while outlining an A Major chord. Note the use of 3rd intervals from the previous chapter.

Example 8d:

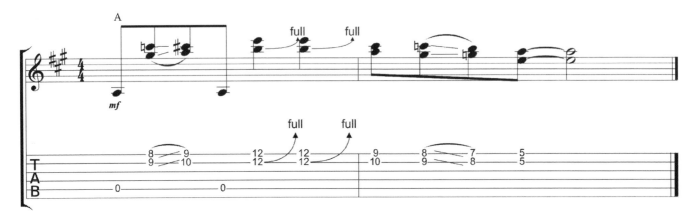

Another common idea taken from pedal steel players is to bend one note and hold it while playing other notes.

Example 8e:

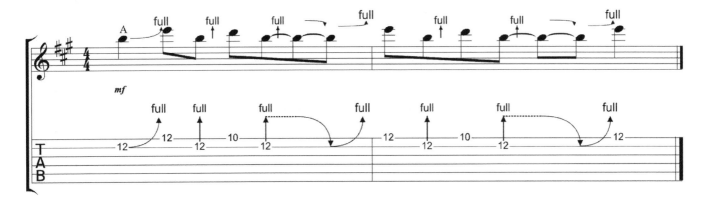

The following example bends the b7 on the B string (G) up to the root (A). This is played against the 3rd (C#) and the 9th (B).

Example 8f:

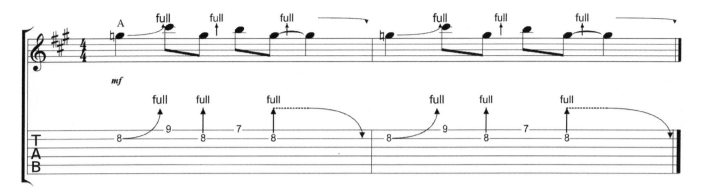

The next lick combines some of the previous ideas to create a line that would work in any solo.

Example 8g:

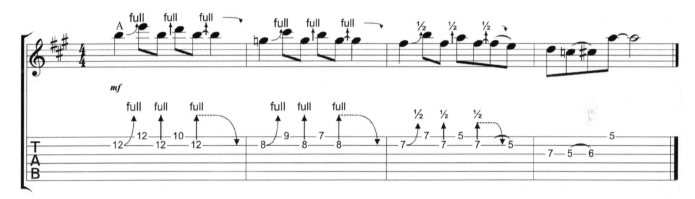

Here's an idea that combines the 6ths from the previous chapter with the pedal steel-inspired bend from the first example.

Example 8h:

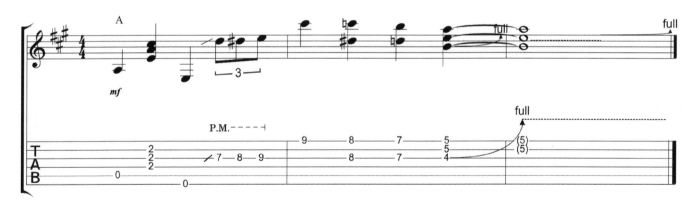

We can also use these bends at the *top* of the melody and place the static notes at the bottom.

Here's another way to play an A chord. Hold the notes on the A and D strings static and bend the note on the G string with the 1st finger.

Steel Bend 2-3

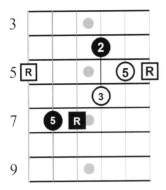

Example 9i:

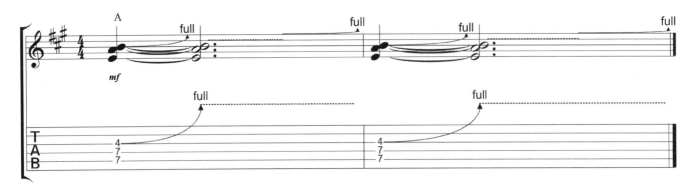

Here's another great way to use this concept, with the b7 and 3rd on the bottom and bending the 5th up to the 6th.

Steel Bend 5-6

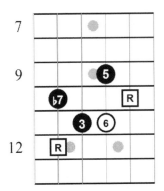

When used in context, this is a great way to lead from A to D.

Example 8j:

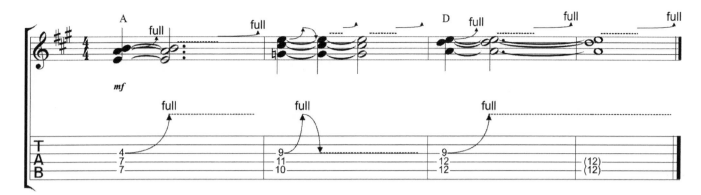

It's also possible to bend notes in the middle of chords, though this requires the use of a B-bender (a mechanical bending system activated by attaching the strap to a lever inside the strap pin). Numerous companies such as Hipshot and Bigsby make retrofit devices to achieve this sound.

Example 8k:

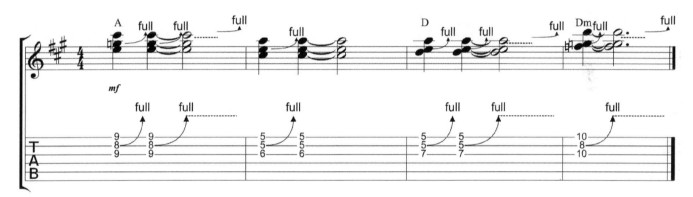

Here's an example that relies on bends found on the G string. Beginning with a bend from the 5th to the 6th on the G, the root and b7th are played against this on the B string. Note the pleasing tension as the F# and G ring into each other.

Measure four extends the idea by moving up to the 12th position and bending the b7 (G) up to the root (A), then playing the 3rd (C#) on the B string.

Example 8l:

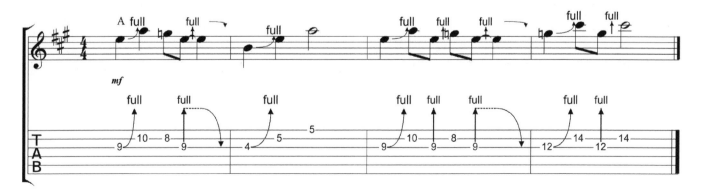

Next up is another idea on the B and E strings, moving down the neck.

Example 8m:

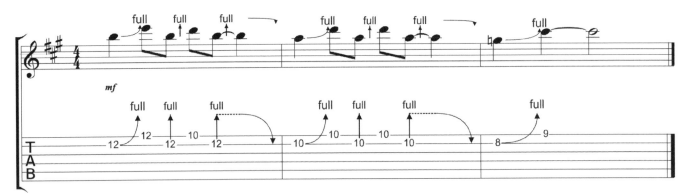

Now the bends are played on the G string, and the melody note is on the high E, allowing you to create some wider intervallic leaps.

Example 8n:

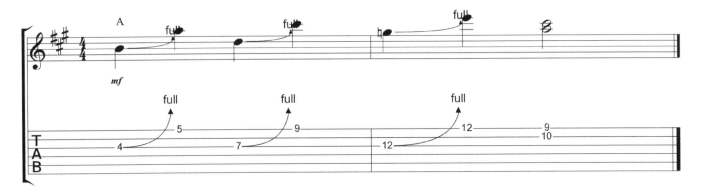

Finally, here's a lick that combines a bend on the G string with a static note on the D. The B (2nd) is bent to a C# (3rd) against a G (b7), creating an A7 sound. Using bends like this is common among the more 'high-tech' country players.

Example 8o:

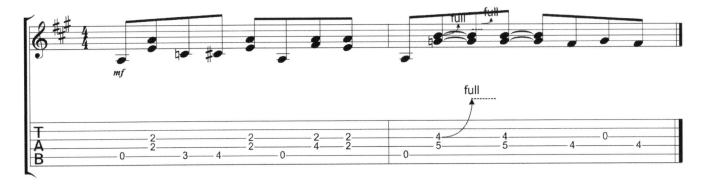

These licks aren't easy, but they illustrate the importance of context. At any given time the country soloist is always aware of the chord they're playing over, so their note choice will have the maximum impact. Nowhere is this truer than with bends.

To demonstrate awareness, here's a little idea played over the G7 - A7 - D7 - G7 progression we've covered previously.

The lick begins by playing over the G7 with a 9 to 3 bend on the B string, with a melody on the high E. This mirrors the idea in example 9e.

In order to outline the A7, we move down to bend the b7 to the root on the B string, as seen in example 9f.

For the D7 chord, we move up to the E shape and bent the 9th up to the 3rd as this position allows you to transition back to the G7 very smoothly.

Example 8p:

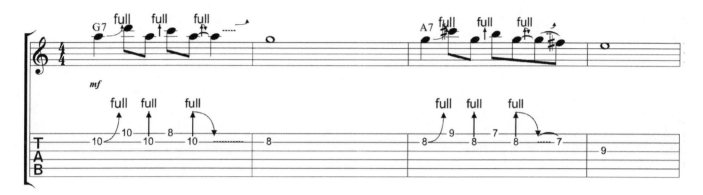

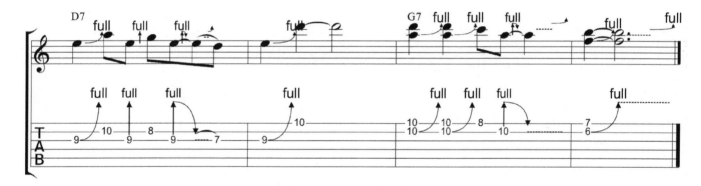

Chapter Nine - Pop Track

One of the true tests of a great country player (or any guitar player for that matter) is their ability to play the *right* part for the song. Often guitarists forget that they'll only be in the spotlight 5% of the time, the rest is about fitting in and adding creatively to the music.

To demonstrate this idea, I've composed a short track for you in the key of E Major, similar to the sort of thing you'd expect a modern country pop star like Miranda Lambert or Carrie Underwood to need guitar on. In this chapter, you'll learn the track one section at a time, and see how best to tackle playing it.

Session gigs are big earners for numerous country guitar players, from legends like Brent Mason and Dan Huff, to hot young players like Daniel Donato and Andy Wood. Understanding how best to fit in a band, and knowing your place is the secret to getting these gigs!

First up, you'll need to learn the chord progression for the intro section. As you can see, it features three chords E, A and B7 (the I, IV, and V7 respectively). I strum these chords on an acoustic to create the pleasing percussive effect you get from a thin pick on a bright guitar.

The only tricky part in this progression is bar eight as it's in 2/4 time, so while you'll be counting to four for the majority of the track, bar eight contains just two beats so (counting from bar 6) you'd count:

1, 2, 3, 4, **1**, 2, 3, 4, *1, 2*, **1**, 2, 3, 4.

This hasn't been done for any reason other than that I like the way it sounds. It has flavours of Alan Jackson's "I don't even know your name", from his 1994 album, Who I Am.

Example 9a:

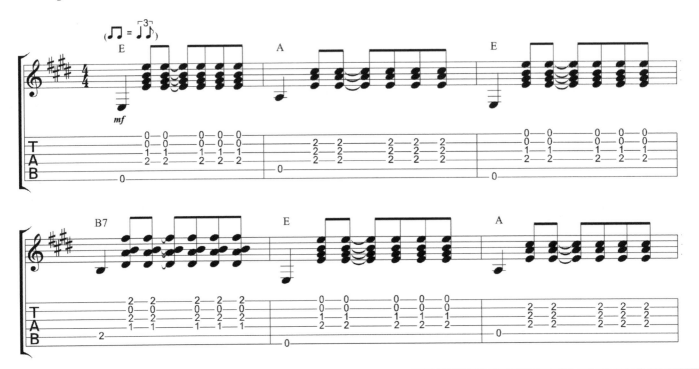

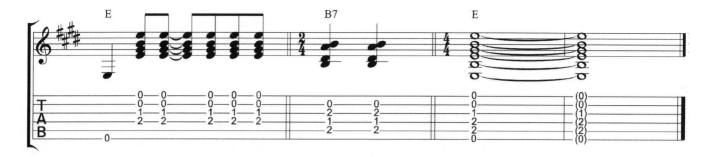

The intro solo features an "anacrusis" or a "pickup bar", this is a short phrase played before bar one to lead you into the song.

Each chord is addressed with pedal steel type bends, though the first three bars do also share a striking resemblance to the E Major Pentatonic scale.

To target the B chord, the soloing position moves down to the E shape at the 7th fret to play a similar bend on the E chord.

Example 9b:

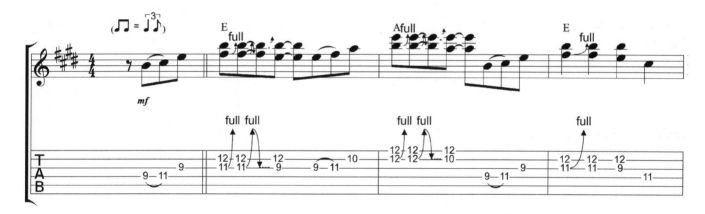

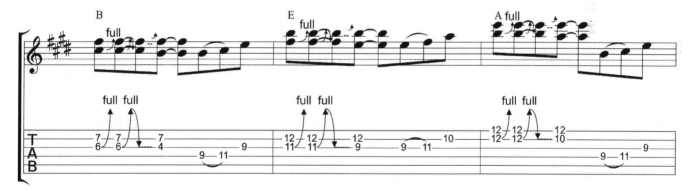

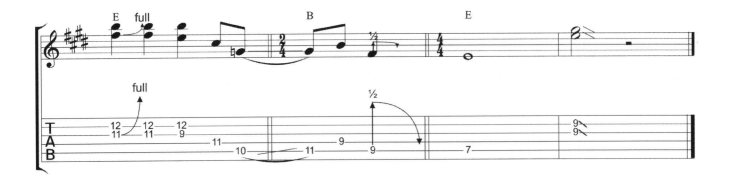

The verse section uses the same three chords as the intro, but now with the IV chord (A) as "home". In order to support a singer, the guitar part is heavily stripped back; just playing chords on the off-beat.

Syncopated rhythms work great in shuffle settings like this.

Example 9c:

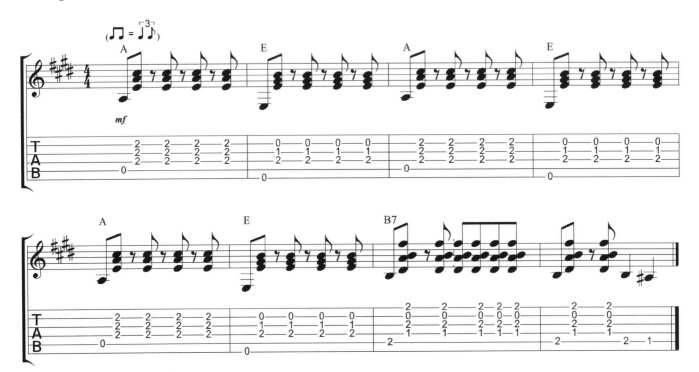

The next example shows an alternative way to play through the verse section, using double stops and bends to outline the chords.

The lick for the E Major chord in bar six is a tricky idea with a bend on the G string, a fretted note on the E string, and then the open E string.

This idea works best on a fixed bridge guitar like the iconic Telecaster. If you're a Stratocaster (or something similar), these bending ideas are often a little out of tune, but pushing on the bridge a little with the heel of the hand to compensate for the movement can help.

Example 9d:

Here's another solo idea that fits over the intro chords (which are now acting as a chorus). The first two bars use the E Major Pentatonic scale, but end on the note A. Bar three features some descending 6ths for the E Major chord, moving to a bending idea to outline the B Major chord.

The next two measure use more 6ths, but this time with palm muted triplets on the D string, before ascending a classic bluegrass melody in the E Country scale. In the 2/4 measure there's a repeat of an earlier pedal steel bend that could be seen as an E Major chord but played against a B Major chord.

Example 9e:

The next example sits somewhere between the rhythm and lead role, mixing double stops based on 3rds that outline chords, with single-note phrases to add variation.

Working through ideas like these will teach you how each one fits into a bigger CAGED shape, and how those bigger forms are used to outline the chord changes.

Example 9f:

There are many ways to approach a track like this but these ideas will give you plenty to chew on. The most important thing is to listen to the greats and see how they tackle songs like this.

Country is still a huge part of the music scene across America, often incorporating many contemporary influences to keep it sounding fresh.

Chapter Ten - Rockabilly Track

As mentioned in Part One, early Country music incorporated a wide influence of styles that then became its own genre; Rockabilly. From Chet Atkins and to the great Scotty Moore, it was the blend of early Rock and Hillbilly music (hence; 'rockabilly') that would form the basis of Elvis Presley's career.

Musicians like Brian Setzer and Danny Gatton brought exciting twists to Rockabilly, but it never lost that early country influence. Players like James Burton kept the sound alive when Scotty Moore left Elvis.

An important part of Scotty's style was how his vocabulary revolved around the basic CAGED barre shapes, most often just the E, A and C shapes. Scotty also used a thumb pick, but there's no need for you to use one as all of these examples can be played easily with a pick (James Burton, Albert Lee, and Danny Gatton certainly don't need a thumb pick!). However, if you've not used a thumb pick, it's worth a try!

Aside from Scotty, other notable players who used thumb picks exclusively include Brent Mason, Jerry Reed, Scotty Anderson, and, of course, Chet Atkins.

This first example is a bare-bones introduction to Travis picking and, while this technique could easily fill a book by itself, the basic skills are relatively simple. As with the examples in Chapter Four, play the notes with downward stems using the pick (notes on the E, A, and D strings) and use the picking hand fingers to play the notes on the G, B, and E strings.

Example 10a:

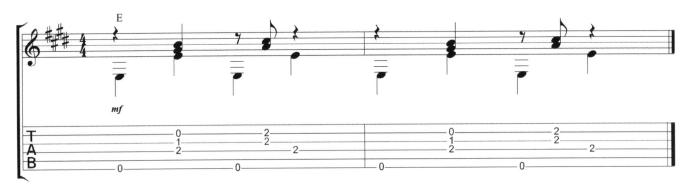

The next example presents an alternative picking pattern that you'll hear from players like Scotty Moore, or modern finger pickers like Buster B Jones.

It's worth learning the bass line separately until the picking motion is automatic, then add the melody.

Example 10b:

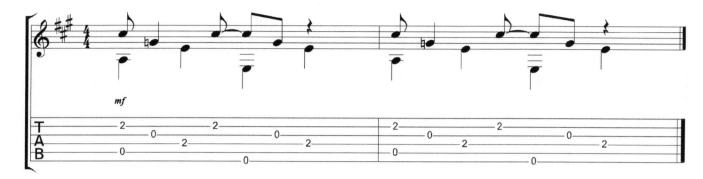

The following idea is a longer example of how to lay down a rhythm track over a twelve-bar blues using picking patterns. Here, however, I stretch the sequence out over twenty-four bars due to the faster tempo.

You'll notice a few tricks being used that help drive the piece forward, such as walking basslines that move between chord changes, but these shouldn't present any problem if learnt slowly. Add some slap-back delay and give it a try!

Example 10c:

When soloing in a setting like this, you may be the only guitar player in a small band, or may playing with a large group of musicians. Either way, using double stops can allow you to both dig in and be heard, while also defining the sound of the chords more effectively in your guitar part.

The following example covers the first eight bars of the tune and uses double stops on the G and B strings to create a nice melody.

Example 10d:

Example 10e features another common Rockabilly approach to lead guitar, which is to *arpeggiate* a ringing chord voicing. As with the previous example, this will add more power than playing single notes.

The voicing used is an extension of the C shape on the top four strings:

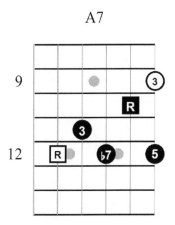

As the track resolves to E Major, I used some more melodic bends with the E Major Pentatonic scale to round it off nicely.

Example 10e:

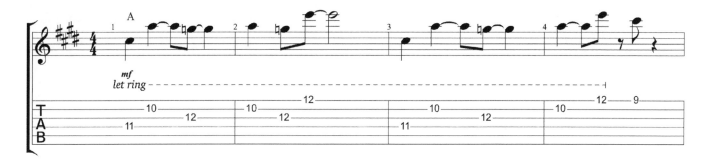

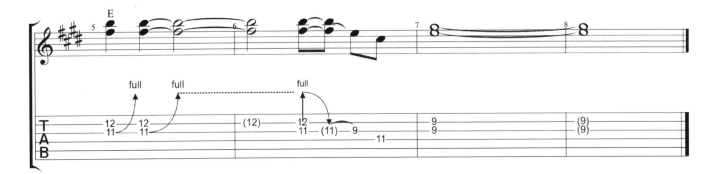

The next lick takes a cue from noted Elvis guitarist (and respected country picker), James Burton to outline the final part of the progression. The playing is visual; moving to the 7th fret for the B chord and then switching to the E Minor Pentatonic scale over the A chord.

Listen to the audio carefully here, as the bent note on the 10th fret is struck repeatedly while being gradually released. For authenticity, the notes should be played staccato (short), and this can be achieved by alternating between the pick and middle finger.

The second half of the lick shifts down the fretboard to the open position and descends the E Blues scale. with an added C# for a bit of colour.

Example 10f:

One the first repeat of the progression, the licks get a little trickier, with more notes and faster position shifts.

Lick 10g begins with some rock-inspired double stops that wouldn't sound out of place in a Chuck Berry solo. In the third bar I play the 6th (C#) and the b3rd (G) together before bending the B string slightly sharp.

The second half of the lick moves down the E Mixolydian scale (with added b3rd) and ends on the b7 (D) of the E Major chord.

Example 10g:

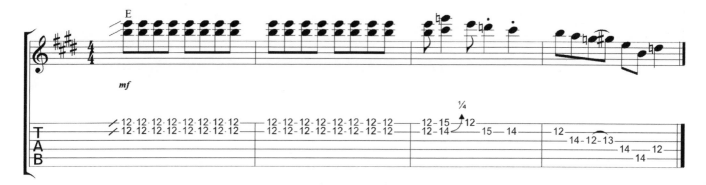

The next lick begins in the E Country scale, but towards the end of the second bar shifts to a series of descending 6ths before resolving with a bend against the open E string.

Example 10h:

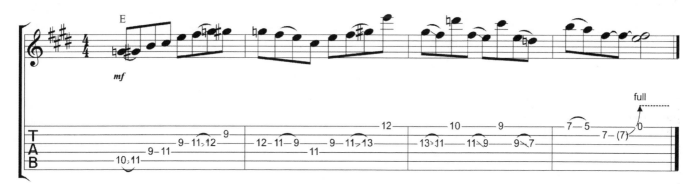

Over the A Major chord, there is a lick reminiscent of Albert Lee. The lick happens in three obvious sections, the descending A Mixolydian idea in the first bar, the open position lick in measure two, and the ascending 6ths towards the end. Albert's style is very position-based, but sounds anything but "boxed in".

Example 10i:

On returning to the E Major chord, you'll find a lick that begins on the low open E string and outlines the E Major Pentatonic scale. To add some spice to this idea, triplets are played on beats two and four, placing a chromatic passing tone between the two notes.

Example 10j:

Finally, over the B Major to A Major chords, I've demonstrated one way to add chromatic tension to a solo. Over the B Major, I approach the 3rd of the chord (D#) from a semitone below, before hitting the 5th (F#). This three-note fragment repeats five times with the note placement falling differently each time.

Over the A Major chord, we use the A Blues scale, before shifting up to end with some classic Mixolydian vocabulary around the E shape.

Example 10k:

Chapter Eleven - Outlaw Track

The final solo in this book is greatly influenced by the Outlaw, and Truck-Driving country traditions. Artists such as Waylon Jennings, Merle Haggard, and David Allen Coe were all well-known for their outlaw sound, so I've drawn on those influences here, along with the neo-traditional sound of artists like Alan Jackson and George Strait.

To mix things up, this track is in the key of G, meaning that the I, IV and V chords will be G Major, C Major, and D Major. First, however, here's the riff which forms the basis of the track. It requires hybrid picking on the double stops and uses notes from the G Mixolydian scale throughout.

Example 11a:

The verse can be played as both an electric and an acoustic part. First up, let's look at the acoustic part which gives you a good idea of the harmony and forms a twelve-bar blues pattern in G. The secret here is that the strumming pattern helps drive the music forward without getting in the way of the other instruments.

Example 11b:

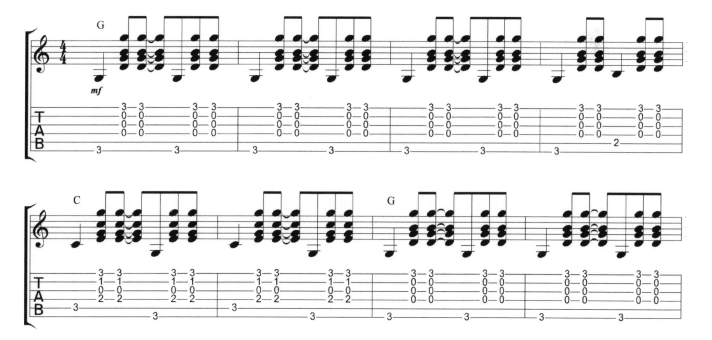

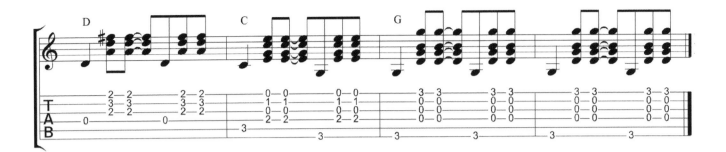

Next, the electric part draws influence from the riff in the intro.

Over the C Major chord, the same basic idea is used, but this time one string set higher. The second half of the bar slides up to play around the G shape.

Over the D, I've played a Dadd11 chord (which is actually just an open C Major chord moved up two frets). An 'add 11' chord is where the (or 11th) is *added* to a Major chord (as opposed to a sus chord, where the 4th *replaces* the 3rd).

Example 11c:

There's a short bridge section before the solo starts. First up, take a look at the acoustic part and simply strum through the chords to get to grips with the changes.

Example 11d:

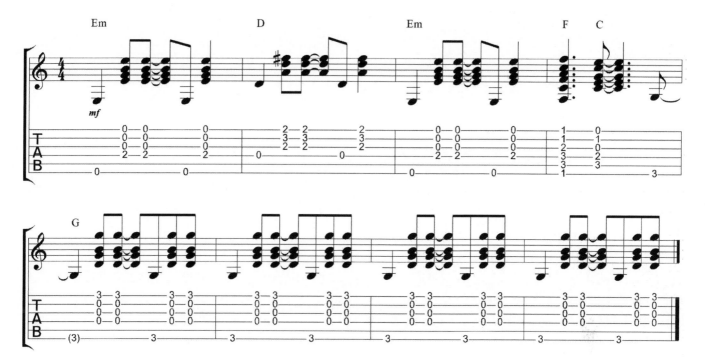

The electric guitar part is more reserved in this section, sticking tightly to the chords and using the Dadd11 from the previous section.

Example 11e:

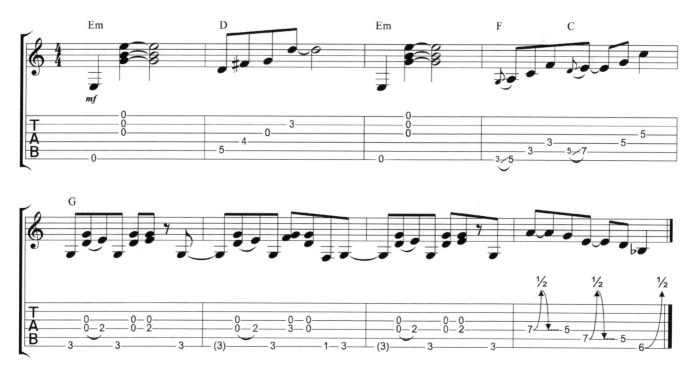

The first lick of the solo outlines a G Major chord, beginning with a pedal steel-inspired bend around the 10th fret, bending the 2nd up to the 3rd, and playing the 5th on the high E string.

The second half of the lick shifts down the neck using 3rds on the G and B strings to end the lick in the E shape. The lick here uses a typical blend of the Minor Pentatonic with an added Major 3rd.

Example 11f:

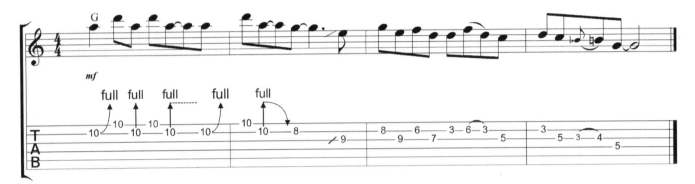

The second part of the solo moves to the C Major chord and back to the G Major. To outline the C Major, I've moved up to the 8th fret area (E shape) and hammered from the b3rd to the 3rd and used the C Mixolydian scale to outline the sound of the chord.

The second part of the lick moves back to G Major and is outlined with some descending 6ths from the G Mixolydian scale.

Example 11g:

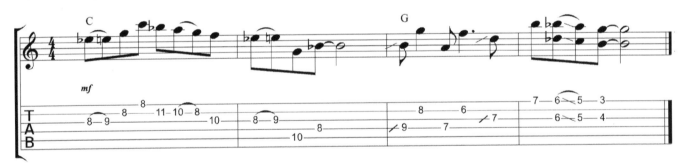

The next two bars move from D Major to C Major. To highlight this change, I begin in the A shape, and slide from the b3rd (F) to the 3rd (F#) of D. The rest of this bar uses notes from the D Mixolydian scale before sliding up to the 3rd of C (E) and ascending the C Major Pentatonic scale.

The second half of the lick is typical of hot country players like Johnny Hiland, with 6ths played on the A and G strings while bending the higher note a scale tone.

Example 11h:

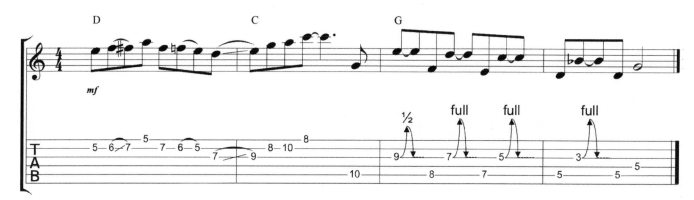

The repeat begins up at the 12th fret, with the G Major Pentatonic scale. The second half of the lick begins around the A shape with more b3rd to 3rd movements.

Example 11i:

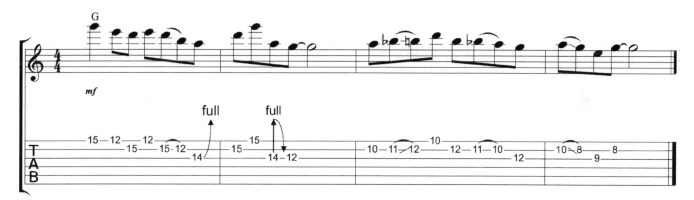

The next lick uses two positions in C Major, beginning with the D shape, before transitioning up to the C shape in the second bar.

The second half of the lick is over a G Major chord, and moves to the E shape high on the neck, bending from the b7 to the root and playing the 3rd on the high E string.

Example 11j:

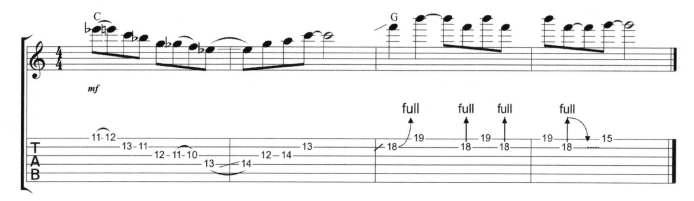

The following lick outlines the D Major and C Major chords before resolving to G Major to end. It begins in the same way as the idea on the C Major chord, is now played one tone higher to fit the D Major. The second bar ends with a classic bluegrass cliché played numerous times.

Example 11k:

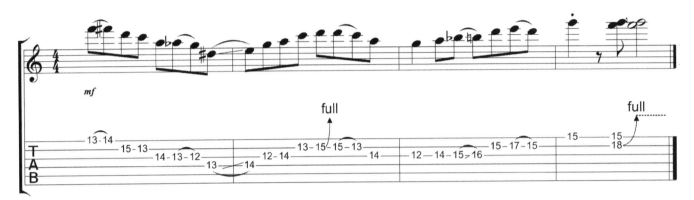

The final lick outlines the chords in the bridge with double stops and pedal steel-type bends. The last two bars require attention as you must hold notes on both the G and B strings while playing different notes on the high E string.

Example 11l:

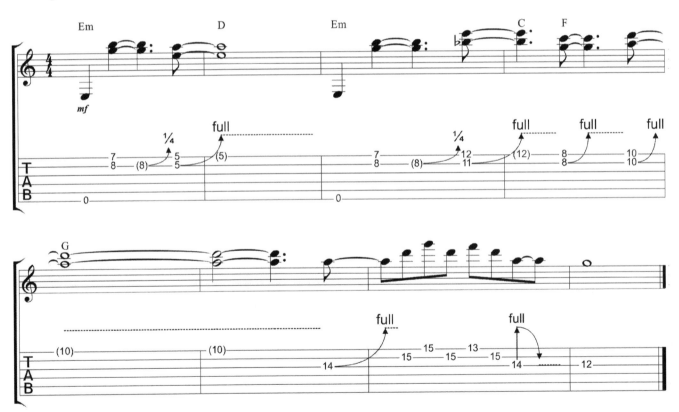

Conclusion

After working through the ideas in this book, you will be well on your way to playing great country guitar. Taking these concepts to the next level will require practice, so I'd like to offer you some tips to help you focus on the things that I feel matter the most in your playing life.

Music isn't about speed; it's about moving people. Sometimes this will require playing fast, perhaps to convey excitement… but *tone* is always king. Spend time listening to the notes you're playing and how they *sound*. Compare the projection heard by Gypsy guitarists, to picking lightly with the tip of the pick. Set a clean tone on your amp and experiment with different picks, dynamics, and picking directions. I find I can get a particularly strong tone by pushing the pick through the string, down towards the pickup.

Timing is also incredibly important. Outside of practicing to the tracks given, use a metronome and train *your foot* to tap on every beat will help your rhythm and phrasing tremendously in the long run.

Remember; the foot taps in time with the click and you *play to the foot*. You aren't tapping along to what you're playing! The pulse is the lifeblood of the music, and your foot will tell you where that is.

Also try practicing with the metronome clicking on beats 2 and 4, like a snare playing on the backbeat. This is especially useful when for faster tempos as your foot won't be moving like a Heavy Metal bass drummer! This feels awkward at first but will help your time keeping immeasurably.

Finally, Here's a suggested listening list of some essential country records for any collection. The beauty of a genre with so much history is that you'll find many 'best of' collections for a great price, so don't be afraid to give some of them a shot.

Alan Jackson - The Greatest Hits Collection
Albert Lee - Live at the Iridium
Andy Wood - Caught Between the Truth and a Lie
Brad Paisley - Time Well Wasted
Brent Mason - Hot Wired
Buck Owens - The Very Best of Buck Owens - Vol. 1
Buddy Emmons - Amazing Steel Guitar
Chet Atkins - The Essential Chet Atkins
Ernest Tubb - Texas Troubadour
Hank Williams - The Best of Hank Williams
The Hellecasters - The Return of The Hellecasters
The Hot Club of Cowtown - What Makes Bob Holler
Jerry Reed - The Unbelievable Guitar and Voice of Jerry Reed
Keith Urban - Days Go By
Maddie & Tae - Start Here
Merle Haggard - The Very Best of Merle Haggard
Merle Travis - Sixteen Tons
Pistol Annies - Annie Up
The Time Jumpers - The Time Jumpers

Good luck with your journey, I hope you've enjoyed these first steps, and I look forward to seeing you at the other end.

Other Books from Fundamental Changes

The Complete Guide to Playing Blues Guitar Book One: Rhythm Guitar

The Complete Guide to Playing Blues Guitar Book Two: Melodic Phrasing

The Complete Guide to Playing Blues Guitar Book Three: Beyond Pentatonics

The Complete Guide to Playing Blues Guitar Compilation

The CAGED System and 100 Licks for Blues Guitar

Fundamental Changes in Jazz Guitar: The Major ii V I

Minor ii V Mastery for Jazz Guitar

Jazz Blues Soloing for Guitar

Guitar Scales in Context

Guitar Chords in Context

Jazz Guitar Chord Mastery

Complete Technique for Modern Guitar

Funk Guitar Mastery

The Complete Technique, Theory and Scales Compilation for Guitar

Sight Reading Mastery for Guitar

Rock Guitar Un-CAGED: The CAGED System and 100 Licks for Rock Guitar

The Practical Guide to Modern Music Theory for Guitarists

Beginner's Guitar Lessons: The Essential Guide

Chord Tone Soloing for Jazz Guitar

Heavy Metal Rhythm Guitar

Heavy Metal Lead Guitar

Exotic Pentatonic Soloing for Guitar

Heavy Metal Rhythm Guitar

Progressive Metal Guitar

Voice Leading Jazz Guitar

The Complete Jazz Soloing Compilation

The Jazz Guitar Chords Compilation

Fingerstyle Blues Guitar

The Complete DADGAD Guitar Method

About Levi Clay

Since graduating from the University of East London with qualifications in both performance, and education, Levi Clay has been an unstoppable force on the international guitar scene.

Working as a writer, teacher, transcriber, journalist, and entertainer for various outlets, it only makes sense that Levi's musical passions are as varied as his skillset.

Having travelled the world as a writer, Levi is still a regular contributor for Guitar Interactive Magazine, both as an on-screen personality and ghost writer.

As a teacher, Levi is well known for his monthly Beyond Blues column for Premier Guitar Magazine, along with his selection of DVD releases for LickLibrary.com. He still maintains a select group of students from all over the world via Skype.

His work as a transcriber has kept him relevant and in demand, completing work for various magazines, publishers, artists, and websites.

Releasing two albums in 2015 ("Out of the Ashes", and "Into the Whisky") via a successful crowdfund initiative, Levi continues to connect directly with his fans and followers via Patreon and YouTube.

Be Social:

For over 250 Free Guitar Lessons with Videos Check out:
www.fundamental-changes.com

Fundamental Changes Twitter: **@guitar_joseph**
Levi Clay Twitter: **@LeviClay88**

Over 7500 fans on Facebook: **FundamentalChangesInGuitar**
Instagram: **FundamentalChanges**

Printed in Great Britain
by Amazon